CHRISTIANITY

AND POWER POLITICS

CHRISTIANITY
AND POWER POLITICS

BY

Reinhold Niebuhr

ARCHON BOOKS
1969

SBN: 208 00740 7
LIBRARY OF CONGRESS CATALOG CARD NUMBER: 69-12421
PRINTED IN THE UNITED STATES OF AMERICA

CONTENTS

CONTENTS

PREFACE

The chapters of this volume are occasional essays, some of which have been previously published in journals of Britain and the United States. While they deal with many subjects, some of them purely secular and political, the unity of the volume is established by the common thesis which underlies the approach to various political issues. This thesis is that modern Christian and secular perfectionism, which places a premium upon non-participation in conflict, is a very sentimentalized version of the Christian faith and is at variance with the profoundest insights of the Christian religion.

The "liberal culture" of modern bourgeois civilization has simply and sentimentally transmuted the supra-historical ideals of perfection of the gospel into simple historical possibilities. In consequence it defines the good man and the good nation as the man and nation which avoid conflict. Sometimes it merely insists that violent conflict must be avoided. But this finally comes to the same thing because the foe may always threaten us with violent reaction to our non-violent forms of pressure, in which case we must desist from pressing our cause or cease to be "good." It is the thesis of these essays that modern liberal perfectionism actually distills moral perversity out of its moral absolutes. It is unable to make significant distinctions between tyranny and freedom because it can find no democracy pure enough to deserve its devotion; and in any case it can find none which is not involved in conflict, in its effort to defend itself against tyranny. It is unable to distinguish between the peace of capitulation to tyranny and the peace of the Kingdom of God. It does not realize that its effort to make the peace of the Kingdom of God into a simple historical possibility must inevitably result in placing a premium upon surrender to evil, because the alternative course involves men and nations in conflict, or runs the risk, at least, of involving them in conflict.

The theological essays in this volume are meant

to prove that this kind of perfectionism is bad religion, however much it may claim the authority of the Sermon on the Mount. The political essays are designed to prove that it is bad politics and that it helps to make the democratic nations weak and irresolute before a resolute and terrible foe.

Some of the essays in this volume are obviously "dated." They have been included despite this fact because in some cases the prophecies which they contained have been all too fully fulfilled, while in other cases they have been proved wrong by current events because they did not measure the tragedy of this era in sufficient depth.

REINHOLD NIEBUHR

Union Theological Seminary.
New York.
August, 1940.

ACKNOWLEDGMENTS

I am indebted to the following magazines for permission to reprint material, in revised form in several instances, which appeared originally in the following journals:

To *The Christian Century* for "Hitler and Buchman"

To *The Nation* for "Idealists as Cynics"; "Peace and the Liberal Illusion"; "Greek Tragedy and Modern Politics"; "Ideology and Pretense"; "An End to Illusions"

To *The New Statesman and Nation* (London) for "Synthetic Barbarism," which has been completely rewritten for inclusion in this book

To *Radical Religion* for "The False Answers to Our Unsolved Problems"

To *Scribner's* for "Modern Utopians"

To *The Christian Register* for "Optimism, Pessimism and Religious Faith," first delivered as the Ware Lecture before the American Unitarian Association

To *The Student World* for "The Christian Church in a Secular Age," first delivered as an address before the Oxford Conference on the Church, Community and State, and then published in *The Student World*, organ of the World Student Christian Federation.

I should also like to express my indebtedness to Mr. W. L. Savage of Charles Scribner's Sons for invaluable aid in compiling these essays.

REINHOLD NIEBUHR

WHY THE CHRISTIAN CHURCH
IS NOT PACIFIST

Whenever the actual historical situation sharpens the issue, the debate whether the Christian Church is, or ought to be, pacifist is carried on with fresh vigor both inside and outside the Christian community. Those who are not pacifists seek to prove that pacifism is a heresy; while the pacifists contend, or at least imply, that the Church's failure to espouse pacifism unanimously can only be interpreted as apostasy, and must be attributed to its lack of courage or to its want of faith.

There may be an advantage in stating the thesis, with which we enter this debate, immediately. The thesis is, that the failure of the Church to espouse pacifism is not apostasy, but is derived from an understanding of the Christian Gospel which refuses simply to equate the Gospel with the "law of love." Christianity is not simply a new law, namely, the law of love. The finality of Christianity cannot be proved, by analyses which seek to reveal that the law of love is stated more unambiguously and perfectly in the life and teachings of Christ than anywhere else. Christianity is a religion which measures the total dimension of human existence not only in terms of the final norm of human conduct, which is expressed in the law of love, but also in terms of the fact of sin. It recognizes that the same man who can become his true self only by striving infinitely for self-realization beyond himself is also inevitably involved in the sin of infinitely making his partial and narrow self the true end of existence. It believes, in other words, that though Christ is the true norm (the "second Adam") for every man, every man is also in some sense a crucifier of Christ.

The good news of the gospel is not the law that we ought to love one another. The good news of the gospel is that there is a resource of divine mercy which is able to overcome a contradiction within our own souls, which we cannot ourselves overcome. This contradiction is that, though we know we ought to love our neighbor as ourself, there is a "law in our members which wars against the law that is in our mind," so that, in fact, we love ourselves more than our neighbor.

The grace of God which is revealed in Christ is regarded by Christian faith as, on the one hand, an actual "power of righteousness" which heals the contradiction within our hearts. In that sense Christ defines the actual possibilities of human existence. On the other hand, this grace is conceived as "justification," as pardon rather than power, as the forgiveness of God, which is vouchsafed to man despite the fact that he never achieves the full measure of Christ. In that sense Christ is the "impossible possibility." Loyalty to him means realization in intention, but does not actually mean the full realization of the measure of Christ. In this doctrine of forgiveness and justification, Christianity measures the full seriousness of sin as a permanent factor in human history. Naturally, the doctrine has no meaning for modern secular civilization, nor for the secularized and moralistic versions of Christianity. They cannot understand the doctrine precisely because they believe there is some fairly simple way out of the sinfulness of human history.

It is rather remarkable that so many modern Christians should believe that Christianity is primarily a "challenge" to man to obey the law of Christ; whereas it is, as a matter of fact, a religion which deals realistically with the problem presented by the violation of this law. Far from believing that the ills of the world could be set right "if only" men

3

obeyed the law of Christ, it has always regarded the problem of achieving justice in a sinful world as a very difficult task. In the profounder versions of the Christian faith the very utopian illusions, which are currently equated with Christianity, have been rigorously disavowed.

Nevertheless, it is not possible to regard pacifism simply as a heresy. In one of its aspects modern Christian pacifism is simply a version of Christian perfectionism. It expresses a genuine impulse in the heart of Christianity, the impulse to take the law of Christ seriously and not to allow the political strategies, which the sinful character of man makes necessary, to become final norms. In its profounder forms this Christian perfectionism did not proceed from a simple faith that the "law of love" could be regarded as an alternative to the political strategies by which the world achieves a precarious justice. These strategies invariably involve the balancing of power with power; and they never completely escape the peril of tyranny on the one hand, and the peril of anarchy and warfare on the other.

In medieval ascetic perfectionism and in Protestant sectarian perfectionism (of the type of Meno Simons, for instance) the effort to achieve a standard of perfect love in individual life was not presented as a political alternative. On the contrary, the political problem and task were specifically disavowed. This

4

perfectionism did not give itself to the illusion that it had discovered a method for eliminating the element of conflict from political strategies. On the contrary, it regarded the mystery of evil as beyond its power of solution. It was content to set up the most perfect and unselfish individual life as a symbol of the Kingdom of God. It knew that this could only be done by disavowing the political task and by freeing the individual of all responsibility for social justice.

It is this kind of pacifism which is not a heresy. It is rather a valuable asset for the Christian faith. It is a reminder to the Christian community that the relative norms of social justice, which justify both coercion and resistance to coercion, are not final norms, and that Christians are in constant peril of forgetting their relative and tentative character and of making them too completely normative.

There is thus a Christian pacifism which is not a heresy. Yet most modern forms of Christian pacifism are heretical. Presumably inspired by the Christian gospel, they have really absorbed the Renaissance faith in the goodness of man, have rejected the Christian doctrine of original sin as an outmoded bit of pessimism, have reinterpreted the Cross so that it is made to stand for the absurd idea that perfect love is guaranteed a simple victory over the world, and have rejected all other profound elements of the Christian gospel as "Pauline" accretions which must

5

be stripped from the "simple gospel of Jesus." This form of pacifism is not only heretical when judged by the standards of the total gospel. It is equally heretical when judged by the facts of human existence. There are no historical realities which remotely conform to it. It is important to recognize this lack of conformity to the facts of experience as a criterion of heresy.

All forms of religious faith are principles of interpretation which we use to organize our experience. Some religions may be adequate principles of interpretation at certain levels of experience, but they break down at deeper levels. No religious faith can maintain itself in defiance of the experience which it supposedly interprets. A religious faith which substitutes faith in man for faith in God cannot finally validate itself in experience. If we believe that the only reason men do not love each other perfectly is because the law of love has not been preached persuasively enough, we believe something to which experience does not conform. If we believe that if Britain had only been fortunate enough to have produced 30 per cent instead of 2 per cent of conscientious objectors to military service, Hitler's heart would have been softened and he would not have dared to attack Poland, we hold a faith which no historic reality justifies.

6

Such a belief has no more justification in the facts of experience than the communist belief that the sole cause of man's sin is the class organization of society and the corollary faith that a "classless" society will be essentially free of human sinfulness. All of these beliefs are pathetic alternatives to the Christian faith. They all come finally to the same thing. They do not believe that man remains a tragic creature who needs the divine mercy as much at the end as at the beginning of his moral endeavors. They believe rather that there is some fairly easy way out of the human situation of "self-alienation." In this connection it is significant that Christian pacifists, rationalists like Bertrand Russell, and mystics like Aldous Huxley, believe essentially the same thing. The Christians make Christ into the symbol of their faith in man. But their faith is really identical with that of Russell or Huxley.

The common element in these various expressions of faith in man is the belief that man is essentially good at some level of his being. They believe that if you can abstract the rational-universal man from what is finite and contingent in human nature, or if you can only cultivate some mystic-universal element in the deeper levels of man's consciousness, you will be able to eliminate human selfishness and the consequent conflict of life with life. These rational or

7

mystical views of man conform neither to the New Testament's view of human nature nor yet to the complex facts of human experience.

In order to elaborate the thesis more fully, that the refusal of the Christian Church to espouse pacifism is not apostasy and that most modern forms of pacifism are heretical, it is necessary first of all to consider the character of the absolute and unqualified demands which Christ makes and to understand the relation of these demands to the gospel.

II

It is very foolish to deny that the ethic of Jesus is an absolute and uncompromising ethic. It is, in the phrase of Ernst Troeltsch, an ethic of "love universalism and love perfectionism." The injunctions "resist not evil," "love your enemies," "if ye love them that love you what thanks have you?" "be not anxious for your life," and "be ye therefore perfect even as your father in heaven is perfect," are all of one piece, and they are all uncompromising and absolute. Nothing is more futile and pathetic than the effort of some Christian theologians who find it necessary to become involved in the relativities of politics, in resistance to tyranny or in social conflict, to justify themselves by seeking to prove that Christ was also involved in some of these relativities, that he used whips to drive the money-changers out of the Temple, or that he came "not to bring peace but a sword," or that he asked the disciples to sell a cloak and buy a sword. What could be more futile than to build a whole ethical structure upon the exegetical issue whether Jesus accepted the sword with the words: "It is enough," or whether he really meant: "Enough of this"?*

Those of us who regard the ethic of Jesus as finally and ultimately normative, but as not immediately applicable to the task of securing justice in a sinful world, are very foolish if we try to reduce the ethic so that it will cover and justify our prudential and relative standards and strategies. To do this is to reduce the ethic to a new legalism. The significance of the law of love is precisely that it is not just another law, but a law which transcends all law. Every law and every standard which falls short of the law of love embodies contingent factors and makes concessions to the fact that sinful man must achieve tentative harmonies of life with life which are less than the best. It is dangerous and confusing to give these tentative and relative standards final and absolute religious sanction.

Curiously enough the pacifists are just as guilty as their less absolutist brethren of diluting the ethic of Jesus for the purpose of justifying their position. They are forced to recognize that an ethic of pure

*Luke xxii, 36.

9

non-resistance can have no immediate relevance to any political situation; for in every political situation it is necessary to achieve justice by resisting pride and power. They therefore declare that the ethic of Jesus is not an ethic of non-resistance, but one of non-violent resistance; that it allows one to resist evil provided the resistance does not involve the destruction of life or property.

There is not the slightest support in Scripture for this doctrine of non-violence. Nothing could be plainer than that the ethic uncompromisingly enjoins non-resistance and not non-violent resistance. Furthermore, it is obvious that the distinction between violent and non-violent resistance is not an absolute distinction. If it is made absolute, we arrive at the morally absurd position of giving moral preference to the non-violent power which Doctor Goebbels wields over the type of power wielded by a general. This absurdity is really derived from the modern (and yet probably very ancient and very Platonic) heresy of regarding the "physical" as evil and the "spiritual" as good. The *reductio ad absurdum* of this position is achieved in a book which has become something of a textbook for modern pacifists, Richard Gregg's *The Power of Non-Violence*. In this book non-violent resistance is commended as the best method of defeating your foe, particularly as the best method of breaking his morale. It is suggested that Christ ended his life on the Cross because he had not completely mastered the technique of non-violence, and must for this reason be regarded as a guide who is inferior to Gandhi, but whose significance lies in initiating a movement which culminates in Gandhi.

One may well concede that a wise and decent statesmanship will seek not only to avoid conflict, but to avoid violence in conflict. Parliamentary political controversy is one method of sublimating political struggles in such a way as to avoid violent collisions of interest. But this pragmatic distinction has nothing to do with the more basic distinction between the ethic of the "Kingdom of God," in which no concession is made to human sin, and all relative political strategies which, assuming human sinfulness, seek to secure the highest measure of peace and justice among selfish and sinful men.

III

If pacifists were less anxious to dilute the ethic of Christ to make it conform to their particular type of non-violent politics, and if they were less obsessed with the obvious contradiction between the ethic of Christ and the fact of war, they might have noticed that the injunction "resist not evil" is only part and parcel of a total ethic which we violate not only in war-time, but every day of our life, and that overt conflict is but a final and vivid revelation of the character of human existence. This total ethic can be summarized most succinctly in the two injunctions "Be not anxious for your life" and "love thy neighbor as thyself."

In the first of these, attention is called to the fact that the root and source of all undue self-assertion lies in the anxiety which all men have in regard to their existence. The ideal possibility is that perfect trust in God's providence ("for your heavenly father knoweth what things ye have need of") and perfect unconcern for the physical life ("fear not them which are able to kill the body") would create a state of serenity in which one life would not seek to take advantage of another life. But the fact is that anxiety is an inevitable concomitant of human freedom, and is the root of the inevitable sin which expresses itself in every human activity and creativity. Not even the most idealistic preacher who admonishes his congregation to obey the law of Christ is free of the sin which arises from anxiety. He may or may not be anxious for his job, but he is certainly anxious about his prestige. Perhaps he is anxious for his reputation as a righteous man. He may be tempted to preach a perfect ethic the more vehemently in order to hide an unconscious apprehension of the fact that his own life does not conform to it. There is no life which does not violate the injunction "Be not anxious." That is the tragedy of human sin. It is the tragedy of man who is dependent upon God, but seeks to make himself independent and self-sufficing.

In the same way there is no life which is not involved in a violation of the injunction, "Thou shalt love thy neighbor as thyself." No one is so blind as the idealist who tells us that war would be unnecessary "if only" nations obeyed the law of Christ, but who remains unconscious of the fact that even the most saintly life is involved in some measure of contradiction to this law. Have we not all known loving fathers and mothers who, despite a very genuine love for their children, had to be resisted if justice and freedom were to be gained for the children? Do we not know that the sinful will-to-power may be compounded with the most ideal motives and may use the latter as its instruments and vehicles? The collective life of man undoubtedly stands on a lower moral plane than the life of individuals; yet nothing revealed in the life of races and nations is unknown in individual life. The sins of pride and of lust for power and the consequent tyranny and injustice are all present, at least in an inchoate form, in individual life. Even as I write my little five-year-old boy comes to me with the tale of an attack made upon him by his year-old sister. This tale is concocted to escape paternal judgment for being too rough in playing with his sister. One is reminded of Germany's

13

claim that Poland was the aggressor and the similar Russian charge against Finland.

The pacifists do not know human nature well enough to be concerned about the contradictions between the law of love and the sin of man, until sin has conceived and brought forth death. They do not see that sin introduces an element of conflict into the world and that even the most loving relations are not free of it. They are, consequently, unable to appreciate the complexity of the problem of justice. They merely assert that if only men loved one another, all the complex, and sometimes horrible, realities of the political order could be dispensed with. They do not see that their "if" begs the most basic problem of human history. It is because men are sinners that justice can be achieved only by a certain degree of coercion on the one hand, and by resistance to coercion and tyranny on the other hand. The political life of man must constantly steer between the Scylla of anarchy and the Charybdis of tyranny.

Human egotism makes large-scale co-operation upon a purely voluntary basis impossible. Governments must coerce. Yet there is an element of evil in this coercion. It is always in danger of serving the purposes of the coercing power rather than the general weal. We cannot fully trust the motives of any ruling class or power. That is why it is important to maintain democratic checks upon the centers of power. It may also be necessary to resist a ruling class, nation or race, if it violates the standards of relative justice which have been set up for it. Such resistance means war. It need not mean overt conflict or violence. But if those who resist tyranny publish their scruples against violence too publicly the tyrannical power need only threaten the use of violence against non-violent pressure to persuade the resisters to quiescence. (The relation of pacifism to the abortive effort to apply non-violent sanctions against Italy in the Ethiopian dispute is instructive at this point.)

The refusal to recognize that sin introduces an element of conflict into the world invariably means that a morally perverse preference is given to tyranny over anarchy (war). If we are told that tyranny would destroy itself, if only we would not challenge it, the obvious answer is that tyranny continues to grow if it is not resisted. If it is to be resisted, the risk of overt conflict must be taken. The thesis that German tyranny must not be challenged by other nations because Germany will throw off this yoke in due time, merely means that an unjustified moral preference is given to civil war over international war, for internal resistance runs the risk of conflict as much as external resistance. Furthermore, no consideration is given to the fact that a tyrannical

State may grow too powerful to be successfully resisted by purely internal pressure, and that the injustices which it does to other than its own nationals may rightfully lay the problem of the tyranny upon other nations.

It is not unfair to assert that most pacifists who seek to present their religious absolutism as a political alternative to the claims and counter-claims, the pressures and counter-pressures of the political order, invariably betray themselves into this preference for tyranny. Tyranny is not war. It is peace, but it is a peace which has nothing to do with the peace of the Kingdom of God. It is a peace which results from one will establishing a complete dominion over other wills and reducing them to acquiescence.

One of the most terrible consequences of a confused religious absolutism is that it is forced to condone such tyranny as that of Germany in the nations which it has conquered and now cruelly oppresses. It usually does this by insisting that the tyranny is no worse than that which is practised in the so-called democratic nations. Whatever may be the moral ambiguities of the so-called democratic nations, and however serious may be their failure to conform perfectly to their democratic ideals, it is sheer moral perversity to equate the inconsistencies of a democratic civilization with the brutalities which modern tyrannical States practise. If we cannot make a distinction here, there are no historical distinctions which have any value. All the distinctions upon which the fate of civilization has turned in the history of mankind have been just such relative distinctions.

One is persuaded to thank God in such times as these that the common people maintain a degree of "common sense," that they preserve an uncorrupted ability to react against injustice and the cruelty of racial bigotry. This ability has been lost among some Christian idealists who preach the law of love but forget that they, as well as all other men, are involved in the violation of that law; and who must (in order to obscure this glaring defect in their theory) eliminate all relative distinctions in history and praise the peace of tyranny as if it were nearer to the peace of the Kingdom of God than war. The overt conflicts of human history are periods of judgment when what has been hidden becomes revealed. It is the business of Christian prophecy to anticipate these judgments to some degree at least, to call attention to the fact that when men say "peace and quiet" "destruction will come upon them unaware," and reveal to what degree this overt destruction is a vivid portrayal of the constant factor of sin in human life. A theology which fails to come to grips with this tragic factor of sin is heretical, both from the standpoint of the gospel

17

and in terms of its blindness to obvious facts of human experience in every realm and on every level of moral goodness.

IV

The gospel is something more than the law of love. The gospel deals with the fact that men violate the law of love. The gospel presents Christ as the pledge and revelation of God's mercy which finds man in his rebellion and overcomes his sin.

The question is whether the grace of Christ is primarily a power of righteousness which so heals the sinful heart that henceforth it is able to fulfil the law of love; or whether it is primarily the assurance of divine mercy for a persistent sinfulness which man never overcomes completely. When St. Paul declared: "I am crucified with Christ; nevertheless I live, yet it is no more I that live but Christ that dwelleth in me," did he mean that the new life in Christ was not his own by reason of the fact that grace, rather than his own power, enabled him to live on the new level of righteousness? Or did he mean that the new life was his only in intention and by reason of God's willingness to accept intention for achievement? Was the emphasis upon sanctification or justification?

This is the issue upon which the Protestant Reformation separated itself from classical Catholicism, believing that Thomistic interpretations of grace lent themselves to new forms of self-righteousness in place of the Judaistic-legalistic self-righteousness which St. Paul condemned. If one studies the whole thought of St. Paul, one is almost forced to the conclusion that he was not himself quite certain whether the peace which he had found in Christ was a moral peace, the peace of having become what man truly is; or whether it was primarily a religious peace, the peace of being "completely known and all forgiven," of being accepted by God despite the continued sinfulness of the heart. Perhaps St. Paul could not be quite sure about where the emphasis was to be placed, for the simple reason that no one can be quite certain about the character of this ultimate peace. There must be, and there is, moral content in it, a fact which Reformation theology tends to deny and which Catholic and sectarian theology emphasizes. But there is never such perfect moral content in it that any man could find perfect peace through his moral achievements, not even the achievements which he attributes to grace rather than the power of his own will. This is the truth which the Reformation emphasized and which modern Protestant Christianity has almost completely forgotten.

We are, therefore, living in a state of sorry moral and religious confusion. In the very moment of world history in which every contemporary historical event justifies the Reformation emphasis upon the persistence of sin on every level of moral achievement, we not only identify Protestant faith with a moralistic sentimentality which neglects and obscures truths in the Christian gospel (which it was the mission of the Reformation to rescue from obscurity), but we even neglect those reservations and qualifications upon the theory of sanctification upon which classical Catholicism wisely insisted.

We have, in other words, reinterpreted the Christian gospel in terms of the Renaissance faith in man. Modern pacifism is merely a final fruit of this Renaissance spirit, which has pervaded the whole of modern Protestantism. We have interpreted world history as a gradual ascent to the Kingdom of God which waits for final triumph only upon the willingness of Christians to "take Christ seriously." There is nothing in Christ's own teachings, except dubious interpretations of the parable of the leaven and the mustard seed, to justify this interpretation of world history. In the whole of the New Testament, Gospels and Epistles alike, there is only one interpretation of world history. That pictures history as moving toward a climax in which both Christ and anti-Christ are revealed.

The New Testament does not, in other words, envisage a simple triumph of good over evil in history. It sees human history involved in the contradictions of sin to the end. That is why it sees no simple reso-

lution of the problem of history. It believes that the
Kingdom of God will finally resolve the contradictions of history; but for it the Kingdom of God is
no simple historical possibility. The grace of God for
man and the Kingdom of God for history are both
divine realities and not human possibilities.

The Christian faith believes that the Atonement
reveals God's mercy as an ultimate resource by which
God alone overcomes the judgment which sin de-
serves. If this final truth of the Christian religion has
no meaning to modern men, including modern Christians, that is because even the tragic character of contemporary history has not yet persuaded them to
take the fact of human sinfulness seriously.

v

The contradiction between the law of love and the
sinfulness of man raises not only the ultimate religious problem how men are to have peace if they
do not overcome the contradiction, and how history
will culminate if the contradiction remains on every
level of historic achievement; it also raises the immediate problem how men are to achieve a tolerable
harmony of life with life, if human pride and selfishness prevent the realization of the law of love.

The pacifists are quite right in one emphasis. They
are right in asserting that love is really the law of

life. It is not some ultimate possibility which has nothing to do with human history. The freedom of man, his transcendence over the limitations of nature and over all historic and traditional social situations, makes any form of human community which falls short of the law of love less than the best. Only by a voluntary giving of life to life and a free interpenetration of personalities could man do justice both to the freedom of other personalities and the necessity of community between personalities. The law of love therefore remains a principle of criticism over all forms of community in which elements of coercion and conflict destroy the highest type of fellowship.

To look at human communities from the perspective of the Kingdom of God is to know that there is a sinful element in all the expedients which the political order uses to establish justice. That is why even the seemingly most stable justice degenerates periodically into either tyranny or anarchy. But it must also be recognized that it is not possible to eliminate the sinful element in the political expedients. They are, in the words of St. Augustine, both the consequence of, and the remedy for, sin. If they are the remedy for sin, the ideal of love is not merely a principle of indiscriminate criticism upon all approximations of justice. It is also a principle of discriminate criticism between forms of justice.

As a principle of indiscriminate criticism upon all

22

forms of justice, the law of love reminds us that the injustice and tyranny against which we contend in the foe is partially the consequence of our own injustice, that the pathology of modern Germans is partially a consequence of the vindictiveness of the peace of Versailles, and that the ambition of a tyrannical imperialism is different only in degree and not in kind from the imperial impulse which characterizes all of human life.

The Christian faith ought to persuade us that political controversies are always conflicts between sinners and not between righteous men and sinners. It ought to mitigate the self-righteousness which is an inevitable concomitant of all human conflict. The spirit of contrition is an important ingredient in the sense of justice. If it is powerful enough it may be able to restrain the impulse of vengeance sufficiently to allow a decent justice to emerge. This is an important issue facing Europe in anticipation of the conclusion of the present war. It cannot be denied that the Christian conscience failed terribly in restraining vengeance after the last war. It is also quite obvious that the natural inclination to self-righteousness was the primary force of this vengeance (expressed particularly in the war guilt clause of the peace treaty). The pacifists draw the conclusion from the fact that justice is never free from vindictiveness, that we ought not for this reason ever to contend against a foe. This argument leaves out of account that capitulation to the foe might well subject us to a worse vindictiveness. It is as foolish to imagine that the foe is free of the sin which we deplore in ourselves as it is to regard ourselves as free of the sin which we deplore in the foe.

The fact that our own sin is always partly the cause of the sins against which we must contend is regarded by simple moral purists as proof that we have no right to contend against the foe. They regard the injunction "Let him who is without sin cast the first stone" as a simple alternative to the schemes of justice which society has devised and whereby it prevents the worst forms of anti-social conduct. This injunction of Christ ought to remind every judge and every juridical tribunal that the crime of the criminal is partly the consequence of the sins of society. But if pacifists are to be consistent they ought to advocate the abolition of the whole judicial process in society. It is perfectly true that national societies have more impartial instruments of justice than international society possesses to date. Nevertheless, no impartial court is as impartial as it pretends to be, and there is no judicial process which is completely free of vindictiveness. Yet we cannot dispense with it; and we will have to continue to put criminals into jail. There is a point where the final cause of the criminal's anti-social conduct becomes a fairly irrele-

24

vant issue in comparison with the task of preventing his conduct from injuring innocent fellows.

The ultimate principles of the Kingdom of God are never irrelevant to any problem of justice, and they hover over every social situation as an ideal possibility; but that does not mean that they can be made into simple alternatives for the present schemes of relative justice. The thesis that the so-called democratic nations have no right to resist overt forms of tyranny, because their own history betrays imperialistic motives, would have meaning only if it were possible to achieve a perfect form of justice in any nation and to free national life completely of the imperialistic motive. This is impossible; for imperialism is the collective expression of the sinful will-to-power which characterizes all human existence. The pacifist argument on this issue betrays how completely pacifism gives itself to illusions about the stuff with which it is dealing in human nature. These illusions deserve particular censure, because no one who knows his own heart very well ought to be given to such illusions.

The recognition of the law of love as an indiscriminate principle of criticism over all attempts at social and international justice is actually a resource of justice, for it prevents the pride, self-righteousness and vindictiveness of men from corrupting their efforts at justice. But it must be recognized that love is also a principle of discriminate criticism between various forms of community and various attempts at justice. The closest approximation to a love in which life supports life in voluntary community is a justice in which life is prevented from destroying life and the interests of the one are guarded against unjust claims by the other. Such justice is achieved when impartial tribunals of society prevent men "from being judges in their own cases," in the words of John Locke. But the tribunals of justice merely codify certain equilibria of power. Justice is basically dependent upon a balance of power. Whenever an individual or a group or a nation possesses undue power, and whenever this power is not checked by the possibility of criticizing and resisting it, it grows inordinate. The equilibrium of power upon which every structure of justice rests would degenerate into anarchy but for the organizing center which controls it. One reason why the balances of power, which prevent injustice in international relations, periodically degenerate into overt anarchy is because no way has yet been found to establish an adequate organizing center, a stable international judicatory, for this balance of power.

A balance of power is something different from, and inferior to, the harmony of love. It is a basic condition of justice, given the sinfulness of man. Such a balance of power does not exclude love. In fact, without love the frictions and tensions of a balance of

26

power would become intolerable. But without the balance of power even the most loving relations may degenerate into unjust relations, and love may become the screen which hides the injustice. Family relations are instructive at this point. Women did not gain justice from men, despite the intimacy of family relations, until they secured sufficient economic power to challenge male autocracy. There are Christian "idealists" today who speak sentimentally of love as the only way to justice, whose family life might benefit from a more delicate "balance of power."

Naturally the tensions of such a balance may become overt; and overt tensions may degenerate into conflict. The center of power, which has the function of preventing this anarchy of conflict, may also degenerate into tyranny. There is no perfectly adequate method of preventing either anarchy or tyranny. But obviously the justice established in the so-called democratic nations represents a high degree of achievement; and the achievement becomes the more impressive when it is compared with the tyranny into which alternative forms of society have fallen. The obvious evils of tyranny, however, will not inevitably persuade the victims of economic anarchy in democratic society to eschew tyranny. When men suffer from anarchy they may foolishly regard the evils of tyranny as the lesser evils. Yet the evils of tyranny in fascist and communist nations are so patent, that we may dare to hope that what is still left of democratic civilizations will not lightly sacrifice the virtues of democracy for the sake of escaping its defects.

We have a very vivid and conclusive evidence about the probable consequences of a tyrannical unification of Europe. The nature of the German rule in the conquered nations of Europe gives us the evidence. There are too many contingent factors in various national and international schemes of justice to justify any unqualified endorsement of even the most democratic structure of justice as "Christian." Yet it must be obvious that any social structure in which power has been made responsible, and in which anarchy has been overcome by methods of mutual accommodation, is preferable to either anarchy or tyranny. If it is not possible to express a moral preference for the justice achieved in democratic societies, in comparison with tyrannical societies, no historical preference has any meaning. This kind of justice approximates the harmony of love more than either anarchy or tyranny.

If we do not make discriminate judgments between social systems we weaken the resolution to defend and extend civilization. Pacifism either tempts us to make no judgments at all, or to give an undue preference to tyranny in comparison with the momentary anarchy which is necessary to overcome tyranny. It must be admitted that the anarchy of war which results from resistance to tyranny is not always creative; that, at given periods of history, civilization may lack the resource to fashion a new and higher form of unity out of momentary anarchy. The defeat of Germany and the frustration of the Nazi effort to unify Europe in tyrannical terms is a negative task. It does not guarantee the emergence of a new Europe with a higher level of international cohesion and new organs of international justice. But it is a negative task which cannot be avoided. All schemes for avoiding this negative task rest upon illusions about human nature. Specifically, these illusions express themselves in the failure to understand the stubbornness and persistence of the tyrannical will, once it is fully conceived. It would not require great argumentative skill to prove that Nazi tyranny never could have reached such proportions as to be able to place the whole of Europe under its ban, if sentimental illusions about the character of the evil which Europe was facing had not been combined with less noble motives for tolerating Nazi aggression.

A simple Christian moralism is senseless and confusing. It is senseless when, as in the World War, it seeks uncritically to identify the cause of Christ with the cause of democracy without a religious reservation. It is just as senseless when it seeks to purge itself of this error by an uncritical refusal to make any distinctions between relative values in history. The fact is that we might as well dispense with the Christian faith entirely if it is our conviction that we can act in history only if we are guiltless. This means that we must either prove our guiltlessness in order to be able to act; or refuse to act because we cannot achieve guiltlessness. Self-righteousness or inaction are the alternatives of secular moralism. If they are also the only alternatives of Christian moralism, one rightly suspects that Christian faith has become diluted with secular perspectives.

In its profoundest insights the Christian faith sees the whole of human history as involved in guilt, and finds no release from guilt except in the grace of God. The Christian is freed by that grace to act in history; to give his devotion to the highest values he knows; to defend those citadels of civilization of which necessity and historic destiny have made him the defender; and he is persuaded by that grace to remember the ambiguity of even his best actions. If the providence of God does not enter the affairs of men to bring good out of evil, the evil in our good may easily destroy our most ambitious efforts and frustrate our highest hopes.

VI

Despite our conviction that most modern pacifism is too filled with secular and moralistic illusions to be of the highest value to the Christian community, we may be grateful for the fact that the Christian Church has learned, since the last war, to protect its pacifists and to appreciate their testimony. Even when this testimony is marred by self-righteousness, because it does not proceed from a sufficiently profound understanding of the tragedy of human history, it has its value.

It is a terrible thing to take human life. The conflict between man and man and nation and nation is tragic. If there are men who declare that, no matter what the consequences, they cannot bring themselves to participate in this slaughter, the Church ought to be able to say to the general community: We quite understand this scruple and we respect it. It proceeds from the conviction that the true end of man is brotherhood, and that love is the law of life. We who allow ourselves to become engaged in war need this testimony of the absolutist against us, lest we accept the warfare of the world as normative, lest we become callous to the horror of war, and lest we forget the ambiguity of our own actions and motives and the risk we run of achieving no permanent good from this momentary anarchy in which we are involved.

But we have a right to remind the absolutists that their testimony against us would be more effective if it were not corrupted by self-righteousness and were not accompanied by the implicit or explicit accusation of apostasy. A pacifism which really springs from the Christian faith, without secular accretions and corruptions, could not be as certain as modern pacifism is that it possesses an alternative for the conflicts and tensions from which and through which the world must rescue a precarious justice.

A truly Christian pacifism would set each heart under the judgment of God to such a degree that even the pacifist idealist would know that knowledge of the will of God is no guarantee of his ability or willingness to obey it. The idealist would recognize to what degree he is himself involved in rebellion against God, and would know that this rebellion is too serious to be overcome by just one more sermon on love, and one more challenge to man to obey the law of Christ.

2

THE WAR AND AMERICAN CHURCHES

THE CHRISTIAN CHURCH of America has never been upon a lower level of spiritual insight and moral sensitivity than in this tragic age of world conflict. Living in a suffering world, with its ears assailed by the cries of the miserable victims of tyranny and conflict, it has chosen to identify the slogan "Keep America out of the War" with the Christian gospel.

It is unable to help the needy for fear lest pity for the victims of tyranny imperil its precious neutrality. From every side one hears stories of churches and of church periodicals which will not allow the true story of Japanese aggression in China and of German tyranny in Europe to be presented fully, lest it arouse the "war spirit." If the Pope publishes an account of the atrocities in Poland, Protestant prejudices against Catholicism are aroused in order to discount the record of German frightfulness there. Thousands of Jewish-Christian German refugees look in vain for adequate help and relief from American Christians. In comparison with the magnificent and heroic philanthropic efforts of the Jews to help their brothers, the Christian charity for refugees has never been more than a pitiful little trickle. At the present moment Christian refugees from Germany are being supported by money primarily supplied by Jews. Efforts to secure a hearing for refugees in our churches face the obstacle of fear that personal accounts of injustice might arouse the amiable and gentle souls of the parish to "hatred." Thus the Christian love commandment is equated with blindness to the tragic realities of a warring world. If modern churches were to symbolize their true faith they would take the crucifix from their altars and substitute the three little monkeys who counsel men to "speak no evil, hear no evil, see no evil."

Just as the churches close their eyes to suffering, they drug their conscience in order that they may not be able to make significant distinctions between contending political forces. The discovery, and obsession with, the fact that the nations which have been forced by fateful necessity and moral decision to stand against the worst tyranny which has ever threatened Europe, are also imperialistic and nationalistic and do not come to the struggle with "clean hands," is supposed to be a great contribution of Christian sensitivity to the political and international problem of our day. As if any one ever came to any significant issue in history with "clean hands"! As if any nation which enforces peace within its boundaries had clean hands! As if any court which arbitrates between contending social forces were pure in its impartiality! Does not every court stand upon a particular sociological locus and is not its impartiality partly a genuine achievement of statecraft and partly a pretension?

It is important of course that religion should not involve itself again in a holy war. It is important that Christianity should recognize that all historic struggles are struggles between sinful men and not between the righteous and the sinners; but it is just as important to save what relative decency and justice the western world still has, against the most demonic tyranny of history. Obviously the Nazis could never have gained a position in Europe from which they can place the whole of a continent under their ban if western society were really healthy. Obviously there is decay in the democratic world and there is no certainty that the capitalistic democracies will be able to rescue what is decent and just in their societies, either from internal corruption or external peril. History, however, does not present us with ideals and clear-cut choices.

There was a time when the socialists of Austria rightly declared that the difference between Hitler's and Schuschnigg's fascism was not very great. But when actually confronted with the peril of having Hitler's worse tyranny fastened upon Austria they wisely (though too tardily) decided that the difference might be all-important in that particular moment of history. That situation was symbolic of all historic decisions. The idea that it is possible to find a vantage point of guiltlessness from which to operate against the world is not a Christian idea but a modern rationalistic one. Ever since the eighteenth century modern secularists have been trying to find the specific causes of social sin and to eliminate them. Injustice was supposed to be caused solely by unjust governments or by faulty economic organization of society, or by human ignorance. Democracy was supposed to be the force of righteousness against monarchy. Socialism was assumed to be free of all imperialistic passions while capitalism was supposed to be the sole source of the imperial will.

"If we can't find the real cause of social injustice," said a typical modern recently, "we would be forced to go back to the absurd doctrine of original sin." That remark is a revelation of the scientific "objectivity" of modernity. The Christian idea of original sin is ruled out *a priori*. This is understandable enough in a non-Christian world. What is absurd is that modern Christianity should have accepted this modern rejection of the doctrine of original sin with such pathetic eagerness and should have spent so much energy in seeking to prove that a Christian can be just as respectable and modern as a secularist. Does he not hold to the same absurd dogma of the goodness of human nature and does he not have the same pathetic hope that if only this or that fault in the educational, social, political or economic system is corrected man will cease to be a peril to himself and to his fellowmen?

The difficulty with such optimism in regard to human nature is that it confuses every political issue in the modern world. Modern Christianity, far from offering corrective insights to this optimism, makes confusion worse confounded by exaggerating it. The secularist believes in the gradual emergence of a universal mind. The Christian believes that every man is potentially a Christ. He has forgotten that in the profoundest versions of Christianity, every man sees in Christ not only what he is and ought to be but also the true reality to which his own life stands in contradiction. Christianity does not believe, as the pessimists do, that men are by nature egotists. Nor does it hold with the optimists that egotism can be easily

37

transcended. It believes rather that men are egotists in contradiction to their essential nature. That is the doctrine of original sin, stripped of literalistic illusions.

It cannot be denied that orthodox Christian Churches have sometimes been betrayed into defeatism in politics by the pessimism implied in the doctrine of original sin, particularly when the doctrine degenerated into one of total depravity. When it did degenerate in this way there was no longer any difference between what Thomas Hobbes believed about human nature and what Christians believed. But the defeatism of pessimists is not our problem. The fatuous optimism in regard to human nature in America is a problem. That optimism is compounded of the rationalistic optimism of the French enlightenment and the pietistic optimism of American sectarian Christianity. There is little difference between H. G. Wells' pathetic messianic message, "we need a world-brain" and American Christianity's continued insistence that if only Christ would rule the nations there would be no war. We must undoubtedly overcome international anarchy if we are to survive as a civilization, but if we must wait for a "world-brain," or a universal culture we will perish. And we will perish also if we wait upon Christians perfectly fulfilling the law of Christ.

International peace, political and economic justice

and every form of social achievement represent precarious constructs in which the egoism of man is checked and yet taken for granted; and in which human sympathy and love must be exploited to the full and yet discounted. Universal peace can wait upon neither universal culture nor universal love. There can be in fact no such thing as universal peace, if we mean by it a frictionless harmony between nations and a perfect justice between men. It ought to be possible for western society to achieve a higher degree of social and political cohesion and to avoid complete anarchy. But such a possibility depends upon a degree of political realism which is lacking today in both our religious and our secular culture. It depends upon a realism which understands how tenuous and tentative every form of social peace and justice is.

It is because modern man has no faith which would make it possible for him to escape despair if he looked at the sad and tragic realities of human existence and human nature that he holds on so desperately to the illusion of the goodness of man. Ideally Christianity has a faith in a divine mercy which overcomes the contradictions of human history, which man never completely overcomes on any level of achievement. But as a matter of fact modern Christians, particularly in America, have no other faith than modern secularists. If Europe is evil we will keep up our courage by believing that America is not involved in European disaster. We are as a matter of fact a part of western society and the victory of tyranny in Europe would not only be morally intolerable but ultimately it would challenge our national interests. Nonetheless we seek desperately to prove to ourselves that this is not true. This is the basis of all the hysterical "keep America out of war" movements. Any sympathy for victims of aggression, whether in Finland, Poland or China, is decried as leading to American involvement. Any discriminate judgments between what is still decent in Europe and what is wholly evil and false is discouraged because this also might in the end involve us in war.

In one sense the logic of this isolationism is of course perfectly correct. It is not possible to make discriminate choices in politics without running the risk of ultimate involvement in conflict, because all social tensions may result in overt conflict and all forms supporting one side or the other may have the consequence of requiring a more direct support. The logic of isolationism is plausible enough but the moral implications are intolerable. If it were followed through consistently in the whole of social life each family would seek to build itself a haven of isolation lest it become involved in the horrid realities of political struggle, which are a part of every national existence. American peace as a symbol of the goodness of man can be maintained only at the price of accentuating every vice in American character, particularly the vices of Pharisaism and self-righteousness which have developed in a nation saved by two oceans from a too obvious involvement in international strife and saved by its wealth from a too obvious display of an internal social struggle.

The effort to maintain the idea of the goodness of man by finding some area of human existence which does not betray the conflict of competing egoistic passions too obviously usually ends in a revelation of human self-righteousness. We are happiest if we can prove that other men may be involved in evil but that we are not. Modern communism has degenerated into a pathetic form of this illusion. It attributes imperialism to capitalistic nations but rests secure in the conviction that a socialistic nation, such as Russia, cannot be imperialistic. It preserves this illusion in defiance of all the obvious facts of contemporary history. This communistic fallacy is hardly more pathetic than the vagaries of our Christian, patriotic isolationists who in one moment try to persuade themselves that America is made of different stuff from other nations and in the next moment seek to throttle every impulse of sympathy and every sense of common responsibility which might establish a common humanity among us rather than a unique guiltlessness.

Thus the Christian ideal of love has degenerated

into a lovelessness which cuts itself off from a sorrow-ing and suffering world. Love is made to mean not pity and sympathy or responsibility for the weal and woe of others, it becomes merely the abstract and negative perfection of peace in a warring world.

The moral and political confusion, created by re-ligious and secular perfectionists who do not under-stand the involvement of all mankind in the sinful realities of history, is aggravated by perfectionists' illusions about peace. It has become almost a universal dogma of American Christianity that any kind of peace is better than war. This always means in the end that tyranny is preferred to war; for submission to the foe is the only certain alternative to resistance against the foe.

That the dogmatic assumption that nothing can be worse than war leads inevitably to an implied or ex-plicit acceptance of tyranny is revealed by many cur-rent pronouncements in the religious world. A study conference of the Churches on the international situation held under the auspices of the Federal Council of Churches at the beginning of 1940 de-clared: "We are convinced that there is ground for hope that a just peace is now possible by negotiation. It is important for the welfare of mankind that the conflict end, not in a dictated but in a negotiated peace based upon the interests of all the people concerned."

This statement, which was commended by the

leading Christian journal in America as containing the very essence of Christian counsel in the war situation was completely divorced from all political realities. The fact is that Hitler wanted a negotiated peace from the time he invaded Poland to the time the great offensive began. Being in possession of the continent, with the exception of France, it was obvious that a negotiated peace would have been possible only upon the basis of leaving him in possession of all the loot he had taken. If such a peace had been made the smaller nations, not yet under the Nazi heel, would have been gradually conquered by economic and political pressure. They would have had no power to resist and no incentive to resist, since they could not have looked forward to any aid in stemming the tide of Nazism. A negotiated peace, when the Churches desired it, would have been merely an easy Nazi victory.

The alternative effort to dislodge the Nazis may wreck Europe even if it succeeds, and it may fail and thus come to the same result as premature capitulation through a negotiated peace. This fact is supposed to justify the hysterical demand for peace on any terms. But our American moralists fail to understand that peoples and nations which face an imminent threat of enslavement do not make nice calculations of alternative consequences. There are critical moments in history when such calculations become irrele-

43

vant. Every instinct of survival and every decent impulse of humanity becomes engaged and prompts resistance, no matter what the consequences. The result may be tragic; but only a very vapid moralism fails to appreciate the beauty and nobility in such tragedy and continues to speculate on how much better it would have been to accept slavery without resistance than to accept it after resistance.

Just as the dogmatic insistence that nothing can possibly be worse than war leads to the explicit or implicit acceptance of tyranny, so the uncritical identification of neutrality with the Christian ethic leads to a perverse obfuscation of important moral distinctions between contending forces. *The Christian Century* has consistently criticized President Roosevelt for not being absolutely neutral. It seems not to realize that this means to condone a tyranny which has destroyed freedom, is seeking to extinguish the Christian religion, debases its subjects to robots who have no opinion and judgment of their own, threatens the Jews of Europe with complete annihilation and all the nations of Europe with subordination under the imperial dominion of a "master race."

The Christian Century answers the arguments of those who believe that civilization is imperilled by the victory of Germany with the simple assertion that this cannot be true since it is war which imperils civilization. Recognizing a certain uneasiness of conscience among Americans it counsels them to hold firm to their resolution not to have anything to do with the conflict and seeks to ease their conscience by advising them that the "Protestant conscience" of Holland and Switzerland arrived at the same conclusions. Most of the neutrals of Europe to whose conscience *The Christian Century* pointed were destroyed while it was holding them up as glorious examples.

In its simple moralism *The Christian Century* had failed to illumine the basic problem of international relations. This problem is the necessity of an obvious coincidence between national and ideal interests before nations embark upon the hazards of war. There was no question in the minds of any of the small neutral nations about the decisive character of the present conflict. Most of them hoped that Europe would be saved without their aid. Their vital interests were in every case involved ultimately but not immediately. When they became involved immediately, namely by invasion of the foe, it was too late to serve either national interest or the values of civilization which transcend national interest.

The fact that there must be some coincidence between national and ideal interests to prompt national action in a crisis is an inevitable political fact, but it is morally dubious and politically ambiguous in its import. It is morally dubious because it leaves other nations to carry the brunt of defending a civilization

45

which transcends the mere existence of those nations. Politically it is ambiguous because the vital interests of a nation may be ultimately imperilled without being immediately imperilled. To wait until ultimate perils become immediate means to wait too long.

The Scandinavian nations would have been well advised to offer united resistance to aggression rather than wait for the extinction of the liberties of each. Holland and Belgium sought to ward off disaster by constructing a neutrality program which pretended to find equal peril in the designs of contending imperial powers. The peril was not equal. There was in fact no peril from the one side at all. The consequence of a policy which obscured the real facts was the invasion of these nations and the break-through of the German army into France. America is of course in the same position. It pretended that its vital interests would be no more endangered by a German victory than by an Allied one. The real situation is that both the ultimate cause of civilization and our own vital interests are much more seriously imperilled by Germany than the Allies. Since the victory of the German armies in Holland, Belgium and France we have gradually awakened to this fact, but probably too late.

In other words the neutrality policy which *The Christian Century* and its kind have praised as representing some kind of Christian ultimate is not only bad morals but bad politics. It represents the cardinal

46

weakness of democracy in facing the perils of tyranny. Democracy, which must take account of the fears and apprehensions of the common people as dictatorships need not, cannot act in time. It can act in time only if it has leaders who are willing and able to anticipate perils which the common man cannot see. By the time the man in the street sees how great the peril is, the danger is so imminent as to make adequate defense preparations impossible.

This natural weakness of democracy as a form of government when dealing with foreign policy is aggravated by liberalism as the culture which has informed the life of the democratic nations. In this liberalism there is little understanding of the depth to which human malevolence may sink and the heights to which malignant power may rise. Some easy and vapid escape is sought from the terrors and woes of a tragic era.

The fact is that moralistic illusions of our liberal culture have been so great and its will-to-live has been so seriously enervated by a confused pacifism, in which Christian perfectionism and bourgeois love of ease have been curiously compounded, that our democratic world does not really deserve to survive. It may not survive. If it does it will be only because it came to its senses in the final hour and because the weaknesses of tyranny may finally outweigh its momentary advantages.

47

3

GERMANY AND THE WESTERN WORLD

T HE CONFLICT BETWEEN Germany and the western world is, in a sense, a conflict between pessimistic and optimistic corruptions of Christianity. German fascism has developed upon a soil of Lutheran Protestantism in which Christian pessimism about the sinfulness of man was allowed to express itself without restraint and with such a degree of consistency that all significant distinctions between justice and injustice in the social order were obscured. Luther had a strong sense of the moral possibilities of redeemed human nature in the field of personal relations. He assumed that in these relations it was possible for the Christian to live by the law of love and that the absolute ethic of the Sermon on the Mount was definitive for these relations. In the realm of collective behavior, however, he was a complete pessimist. He saw no possibility of checking the sinful selfishness of men except by the divine ordinance of government. Secular government, "the Kingdom of God's left hand," was instituted according to his doctrine to arrest the anarchy and conflict which resulted from human sin.

Thus the highest possibility in corporate life was not justice but coerced order and peace. Luther was unmindful of the perils of tyranny which reside in every scheme of coerced order; nor did he see to what degree a government or state might represent the principle of order in domestic relations and yet represent the principle of anarchy in the relations of states to each other. Lutheran pessimism therefore produces a political ethic remarkably similar to the secular pessimism of Thomas Hobbes. The similarity springs from very similar conceptions of human nature in Luther and Hobbes. In the thought of Hobbes man was essentially evil and selfish, he was "to his fellow-man a wolf." In Christian thought sinful self-love is never regarded as an essential characteristic of human nature. Man is in essence a child of God. However, Luther's view of human depravity, his belief that the "image of God" had been totally corrupted and was "utterly leprous and unclean" destroyed, or at least greatly imperilled, the paradox of the Christian view of human nature, according to which self-love is "natural" in the sense that it is universal but is not natural in the sense that it represents a contradiction of the true human nature. The Lutheran Reformation is therefore that particular locus in the history of Christendom where the problem of justice is most nearly disavowed. It is therefore no accident of history that Nazi pessimism, with its glorification of force as the principle of order, its unqualified affirmation of the state, its disavowal of all concepts of justice and its rejection of all universal standards of morality, should grow upon this soil.

The western democracies, so-called, are, on the other hand, spiritual children of the Renaissance rather than the Reformation. The Renaissance was an optimistic, rather than pessimistic, reaction to the synthesis of optimism and pessimism of Medieval Christianity. Medieval Christianity was a synthesis of the classical-rationalistic and of the biblical view of man. It was also a synthesis of pessimistic and optimistic views of human nature. In this synthesis optimism was, however, more potent than pessimism. For Roman Catholicism man is a sinner, involved in self-love and incapable of doing good. The infusion of divine grace, however, heals the sinful will of man and enables him to fulfill the law of Christ essentially. Catholicism is optimistic about the redeemed man. Though man is involved in untruth in his natural condition he may know the truth by Revelation.

Though he is given to self-love in his natural state, he is capable of loving God and the neighbor, once sacramental grace has been infused. The Reformation rightly challenged this too simple view of sanctification. It recognized the continued possibility of sin in the life of the redeemed. The difficulty of the Reformation was that it did not always recognize the actual possibilities of good on every level of human achievement, no matter what the corruptions of sin. It did not (at least not in its Lutheran form) see that a theory of total depravity is impossible, that untruth requires a minimal degree of truth to carry it, that injustice is impossible without a minimal degree of justice and that all evil can enter the world only as a parasite of the good.

The Renaissance on the other hand destroyed the Christian paradox from the other side. It was enamored of the tremendous possibilities of the human mind, saw human history as a realm of infinite potentialities, but forgot that it is a realm of evil as well as good potentialities. In both its rationalism and its mysticism the Renaissance thought that it had found methods of extricating the universal man from the particular man, imbedded in the flux of nature and subject to the contingencies of history. It did not realize that human history is involved in the pretension of claiming universal significance for particular and contingent values on every level of human culture and that there is therefore no possibility of eliminating the conflict of interest on any level or that it is not possible to abstract reason from the vitalities of nature and history.

The western democracies do not stand under the Renaissance influence in its pure form. Renaissance optimism has been mediated to the modern world primarily through the Enlightenment and through sectarian Christianity. The French Enlightenment, the Age of Reason, is a particularly vapid form of Renaissance thought. In it the Platonic and Stoic conceptions of reason are supplanted by more naturalistic and Democritean concepts of reason and nature in which the two are practically identified. This means that man looks for the principle of order in his life not in a realm of divine freedom above him but in the realm of natural necessity below him.

As a consequence the fact of human freedom is obscured and the tragic character of human history, in which man is perennially betrayed to use his freedom for destruction as well as construction, is not understood. If man is involved in the disasters of history it is always assumed that there is a comparatively easy method of escape from them. He needs only to return to the order, harmony, justice, equality and equanimity of nature. The philosophical foundation of modern capitalism is the most perfect product of such thought; for the assumption upon which capitalistic complacency rests is that there is a pre-established harmony of nature which guarantees a just relation between all economic forces, if only man does not interfere with the automatic processes of economic life. Unfortunately this philosophy was introduced into modern history at the precise moment when a technical civilization accentuated the historic inequalities of a feudal society and made the conflicts between contending social forces more deadly.

The democratic idealists of the eighteenth century were slightly more realistic and as a consequence the political order which they fashioned achieved a greater degree of justice than the economic order which was based upon physiocratic theory. Even the political order, however, was based upon false assumptions. Democratic liberalism did not trust in the order and harmony of nature but it did assume that the human mind could ultimately arbitrate all competing interests and eliminate all conflict. Modern democracy, inasfar as it rests upon the thought of the Enlightenment, overestimates the rationality of man, thinks that there is a simple path to universal justice and harmony, obscures the perennial element of conflict in human society and disregards the non-rational vitalities of human existence.

Sectarian Protestantism, in distinction to the Protestantism of the Reformation, is also a child of the Renaissance. It is derived from the mysticism of the

Renaissance which in turn was derived from the strain of mysticism in Medievalism. Unlike Reformation Protestantism, sectarian Protestantism is not critical of the perfectionist illusion of medieval Catholicism. It is even more perfectionist than Catholicism. It merely insists that human perfection cannot be achieved by an infusion of sacramental grace but is possible only through a genuine personal crisis-experience by which the individual is renewed and finally made perfect.

Sectarian Protestantism differs widely in some of its characteristics. The perfectionism of John Wesley is not as simple as that of George Fox; and the individualism of the pietists is in striking contrast to the social hopes of apocalyptic sects such as the Anabaptists. They all do have one thing in common. They believe that the Kingdom of God, whether in individual or in social terms, can become an actual historic achievement. This means, in other words, that Protestant sectarianism agrees with all forms of Renaissance thought in regarding human history as an infinite realm of moral achievement without recognizing the possibilities of human sin and destruction upon each new plane of cultural advance. Sectarianism is not as simply rationalistic, and certainly not as naturalistic, as the Enlightenment. It knows that man has a freedom which cannot be levelled to the dimensions of nature and it also knows that his reason cannot be simply extracted or abstracted from will and emotion. But it arrives finally at the same optimistic conclusions about human life and history.

The unbelievable optimism of American political life can be understood only if one recognizes to what degree the perspectives of the Enlightenment and of Sectarianism have been united in America, particularly in recent decades. It is this compound of religious and secular optimism which has made religious life so fatuous in our country, has tempted so many Christians to a pitiless self-righteousness in their attitude toward the suffering peoples of belligerent nations, has persuaded them that it is possible to remain aloof from world conflict if only one holds to that purpose resolutely enough, and has generated a pacifism in which religious perfectionism is compounded with self-seeking prudence into the most unholy Pharisaism of religious history.

If one compares the optimism of America with the pessimism of Germany one is driven to the plausible conclusion that the two most inept nations on earth in the realm of politics are Germany and America; and that they are inept for opposite reasons. In Germany the task of achieving justice was prematurely given up and as a consequence the tyrannical unification of political forces was given religious sanction. In America the task of achieving justice was underestimated. American idealists have never realized how difficult it is to avoid tyranny in the economic order in which a technical civilization aggravates previously given disproportions of power. Even now they do not understand how long and tragic the history of a decaying capitalism is bound to be. They never cease to hope that the inordinate demands of the powerful can be mitigated by making the right kind of moral or religious appeal to the wielders of power. Nor do they understand that in the present moment western civilization may be forced to run the perils of annihilation in order to avoid the danger of capitulation to tyranny. It is significant that the very tyranny which has developed on the soil of religious and political pessimism should remain an unfathomed evil on the soil of religious and political optimism. American idealists think it sufficient to declare that nothing could be worse than war.

It would not be just to hold Lutheran pessimism responsible for all the perversion of political standards which the Nazi state has achieved. Many other factors have contributed to this development. The Hegelian worship of the state as the incarnation of man's universal will, the Nietzschean transvaluation of values and the romantic emphasis upon race and vitality in Herder and Fichte, are all compounded in the Nazi creed. Furthermore, Lutheran Protestantism never ceased to regard as sin what the Nazis raise to the eminence of virtue. It remains true nevertheless

57

that Lutheran pessimism is too oblivious to the genuine achievements of justice which are possible in any political order, despite the fact that the sin of self-interest qualifies every concept and every realization of justice. Consistent Lutheranism does not permit the distinctions between relative justice and injustice, which are the very stuff of political decisions; and its conception of government is at once too negative and too sacrosanct.

It is significant, incidentally, that when Reformation theology was revived in Germany after the World War in what is now known as "dialectical theology" or Barthianism, Karl Barth actually reduced Lutheran pessimism to a new level of consistency and made it even more difficult for the Christian conscience to express itself in making the relative decisions which are so necessary for the elaborations of justice in the intricacies of politics and economics. Karl Barth's present position of uncompromising hostility to Nazism cannot change the fact that his system of thought helped at an earlier date to vitiate the forces which contended against the rising Nazi tyranny.

It would not be fair to leave the characterization of American optimism without some qualifications. There are, or at least there were, some elements of wholesome realism in American life. The political philosophy of James Madison and the concept of checks and balances which entered into our American constitution were based upon a recognition of the perennial influence of interest upon political ideas, of the character of politics as a contest of power, and of the necessity of balancing various centers of power in government against one another in order to prevent tyranny. Some of these insights were derived from Calvinism, which began with a view of human nature as consistently pessimistic as that of Luther and which made the same mistake of giving government an unqualified divine sanctity and pronouncing an absolute *caveat* against rebellion.

However, the Calvinistic doctrine of "common grace" and Calvin's conception of a not totally corrupted reason provided the basis for a positive attitude toward the problem of justice, and the exigencies of Reformation politics in France, Scotland and Holland led to important reservations upon the divine right of government. These reservations were gradually broadened to become the basis of democratic political theory. Despite the aberrations of the Geneva and the Massachusetts Calvinistic theocracies, the contributions of Calvinism to political theory probably exceed those of either Thomism or sectarian Christianity. It is freer of perfectionist illusions than either and yet, in its later developments, it did not

59

give up the task of seeking for justice by using the best methods of neutralizing self-interest in politics and of checking power with power.

In the amalgam of American Protestantism Reformation perspectives were largely engulfed by sectarian and secular viewpoints, particularly in the past half century. For this reason one cannot necessarily expect particularly realistic political insights from Christians who stand in the Presbyterian tradition. Methodists, standing in the perfectionist tradition, may be realists in dealing with political problems and Presbyterians may be as filled with moralistic illusions, in individual instances, as pure sectarians. The contributions made by Calvinism to our political life are frequently preserved with greater loyalty by secular political thinkers, who are unconscious of the source of their heritage, than by those who stand ostensibly in the Calvinist tradition.

Though it has become the fashion among American liberals to speak with cynical disrespect of the British Empire it is true nevertheless that the British have exceeded all modern nations, including our own, in combining moral purpose with political realism. Their traditionalism, most perfectly expressed in the philosophy of Edmund Burke and embodied in the feudal forms of their Church and State, has preserved some of the organic forms of life which a pure rationalism destroys and which the Nazis have sought to re-establish in primitive and destructive terms.

The forces of secularism which have dominated both France and America have never destroyed the Christian ethos in Britain. The Calvinism of Scotland and the quasi-Catholicism of the Anglican Church have both contributed to a political theory and life, in which justice was achieved by a combination of moral and political restraints upon the play of power. British realism was not great enough to understand the threat of the Nazi mania in time. Centuries of security and stability had partly enervated the shrewder political instincts of the nation. Yet on the whole the British achievement in politics remains a monumental one. One shudders to think what may happen to our nation in comparison if recent events thrust imperial tasks upon us from which there will be no escape and for which we have no preparation. We will probably engage in them in terms of alternate cynicism and utopianism, seeking in one moment to disavow the task for the sake of the purity of our souls and in the next to follow the course of "manifest destiny" with purely cynical self-interest.

The utopianism of America and the pessimism of Germany are the two aberrations of modern culture in dealing with the complexities of the political order. Ideally, the necessary idealism and the equally necessary realism can be held together only in terms of a Christian faith which refuses to make sin and self-interest normative but which also understands that human history offers no simple way out to the kingdom of pure love and complete disinterestedness. The way to a just and stable social order lies not in the emancipation of reason from force nor yet in the glorification of force. The unity of man's body and spirit makes the first impossible and the second demonic. The way out lies in a transcendence of reason over force sufficient to regulate, equilibrate, arbitrate and direct the play of force and vitality in social life so that a maximum of harmony and a minimum of friction is achieved. Naturally such a task is too difficult to make perpetual success possible. There will be periods of decay and destruction, such as our own, in which it is necessary to risk the very destruction of civilization for the sake of preventing a tyrannical unification of western Christendom. This is a tragic necessity but if it is not understood we may lose the gains of centuries, while we dream of an ideal international order.

There is no such simple universal order or universal justice as modern rational culture assumed. All forms and orders of history are subject to the contingencies of nature and time. The Nazi glorification of "race" is, in one of its aspects, the cruel vengeance which history has taken upon the neglect of "organic" forms by a rationalistic culture. Reason cannot transcend the organic fact of sex so completely as to create the kind of sex equality of which a utopian feminism dreams. Yet it is important to challenge male autocracy and to accept no inequality between the sexes with equanimity. Man can neither escape the bounds and limits of nature nor yet achieve salvation by glorifying them. No "universal brain," of which H. G. Wells dreams, can completely transcend or eliminate the particularity of social life which is for the moment embodied in the race-nation and the nation-state. Yet the effort to make the state and the nation the final end of human existence results in the most demonic aberrations.

Nazi tyranny represents an attempt to return to the limited forms and the simple vitalities of nature. Since man is more than nature he cannot make such a venture without falling into psychopathic aberrations and destroying the very texture of human culture. But the culture which Nazism threatens to destroy made a more harmless but none the less dangerous mistake of trying to abstract mind from force, reason from interest, and rational form from organic vitality. It committed the error, not only of believing that human history was a gradual emergence of the infinite and universal from the finite and particular but also of obscuring the fact of sin in history. Sin in history is not finiteness and particularity. Sin is the false eternal and the false universal. Man is a sinner not because he is finite but because he refuses to admit that he is. And there is no life which is not involved in this tragic self-deception. This is a factor in history to which modern culture is completely oblivious; and modern Christianity abandoned its own heritage to follow modern culture in this blindness.

4

DEMOCRACY AND FOREIGN POLICY

THE TERRIBLE PLIGHT IN which the democracies have found themselves in warding off the threat of totalitarian tyrannies is partly the consequence of a natural weakness of democratic government in the field of foreign policy. Democracies cannot anticipate the future as do the dictatorships. Hitler has built his superiority of tanks and aircraft by denying the German people the ordinary comforts for a period of seven years. Through these years the welfare of a nation has been subordinated to the task of preparing instruments of destruction. No democratic statesman could have demanded or secured comparable sacrifices. The people are not prepared for such sacrifices for a cause in which they do not believe.

They are ready to make comparable sacrifices when the peril of enslavement is obvious, but that may be too late. A civilized nation, in which the voice of the people must still be heard, cannot subordinate the common welfare for an imperial task. In that fact there is a certain hope for relating democracy to peace. But a civilized nation seems equally incapable of envisaging the perils of enslavement in time to avoid catastrophe. That fact may spell the doom of democracy. The isolationism of America belongs in the same category of political facts as the complacency of the British people during the Munich crisis. In both cases the general public did not understand strategy well enough to know that by yielding to a tyranny now, or by sacrificing allies and refusing them help, it was merely hastening the day when it would have to face that same tyranny with fewer resources.

The general public understands only immediate and obvious and not ultimate perils. Even now there are Americans who think we are safe from Hitler because there is little prospect of his landing an army in New York. It does not see to what degree a triumphant Nazi tyranny can wrest the South American republics from us, can corrupt Latin-American governments, can flood the world market with cheap goods, can combine with Japan to make every American position except our own shores untenable. One element alone in this threat is worthy of particular attention: the peril of a competitor in the world markets who will, for the first time in history, combine slavery with technical efficiency. We have had slavery before but it has been inefficient. We have had technical efficiency before in our modern industrial society. A Nazi imperialism, unifying Europe, exploiting all the resources of a continent with modern skill and the slave labor of subject peoples, will be a new kind of competitor. It will give us a competition which is bound to destroy all the living standards and imperil all the democratic rights which isolationists promise to maintain so confidently if only we stay out of the war.

These ultimate perils the man in the street does not understand. The average person in Britain did not understand that Hitler was given a great bastion at Munich. He thought, rather, that a few million Sudeten-Germans were allowed to return "home" and this return appealed to his sense of justice.

It has been the fashion among liberals to attribute the unbelievable imbecilities of democratic diplomacy to the class interests of the capitalistic oligarchy alone. It is unnecessary and impossible to deny that class interests, symbolized in particularly venal terms by such men as Bonnet in France, did contribute to the long series of diplomatic defeats which the democracies suffered before the outbreak of war. These defeats, however, would not have been possible if the general public had been fully aware of the perils to which its oligarchs were exposing the State. American liberals have had good sport with Chamberlain's policy at Munich and have tried to prove that the Britain of Chamberlain is not worth defending. But they did not understand to what degree the "good people" of Britain, without reference to class interests, supported Chamberlain and that without that support he could not have spoken for Britain in that crisis. Furthermore, they do not realize to what degree they, these same liberals, express a blindness to the perils of Nazi tyranny in America which is identical with the blindness of the British people at Munich.

The defects of democratic government in the field of foreign policy are aggravated by the liberal culture, which has supported democracy in the past two hundred years. This culture is deficient in the "tragic sense of life." It has no capacity to gauge the kind of monstrous evil which the Nazi state incorporates. It is full of illusions about the character of human nature, particularly collective human behavior. It imagines that there is no conflict of interest which cannot be adjudicated. It does not understand what it means to meet a resolute foe who is intent upon either your annihilation or enslavement. This bourgeois liberalism contributed to the weakness and ineptness

68

of the Scandinavian states, waiting one by one as fatted cattle for the slaughterer, refusing to consolidate their forces for fear that they might prompt the terrible enemy to take action against them. This liberalism helped to destroy Holland. The upper business classes of Holland refused even at the last moment to take any precautions against traitors and spies in their midst, for fear of arousing Hitler's ire. Hitler of course counted upon just such fears. They belong to the characteristics of a liberal world which Hitler understands quite well and which give him confidence in his ability to destroy it.

This liberalism imagines that it can sublimate the conflict of life with life until all elements of force have been eliminated from it. It rightly believes in its superiority over barbarism; but it does not know that civilizations must periodically meet the threat of barbarism by an organization of their physical resources, somewhat comparable to that which barbarism is able to achieve. It allows Hitler to build a deadly air force without taking proper counter measures. It speaks fatuously, in its gravest hour of peril, of the ability to resist tanks and guns by moral force. It does not know that civilized life may become too enervated, too luxurious and comfortable, too individualistic and lacking in social co-ordination to face the threat of barbarism.

In the hour of crisis the intellectual critics of the democratic world combine their own kind of complacency with the complacency of the oligarchy. In every civilized world there is an oligarchy which has ruled so long that it is incapable of believing that its rule could be successfully challenged. Like Babylon of old it declares: "I sit as a Queen and shall be no widow and shall never know sorrow." It does not understand that this very complacency justifies the prediction of the prophet: "Therefore in one moment shall her sorrow come." The critics of civilization do not have this kind of complacency. They merely believe that a superior civilization cannot succumb to an inferior one. They speak glibly of the fact that "force has never settled anything in human history."

Sometimes the critics follow counsels of despair rather than complacency. Being utopians at heart, they do not believe that civilization is worth defending, because it is full of injustice of every kind. They forget how much worse the barbarism would be than this unjust society. Every decent person must of course have some appreciation of the plight of sensitive spirits who have for so long rightly criticized the injustices of our society, that they cannot in a moment change their strategy and defend what they have been attacking. But a less utopian culture than the liberalism which has informed democratic society would know that all historic choices are relative. It would realize that even an imperfect pluto-democratic world is still civilization and that the alternative which the Nazis propose is really slavery.

The natural defects of democracy as a form of government and the blindness of liberalism as the culture of democracy combine to make democracy almost defenseless against the concentrated fury which the totalitarian powers are unleashing. The defects of democracy in foreign policy can be overcome only by a leadership which is willing to risk its prestige by words and actions which anticipate the perils to which the State is exposed and which defy the common lethargy of the moment in order to ward off ultimate peril. President Roosevelt has had something of this kind of relationship to the American democracy. He understood Hitler when Chamberlain did not. Unfortunately his dependence upon the good will of the Catholic hierarchy (a dependence which is derived from the intimate relation between the municipal democratic machines and the Catholic Church) prevented him from taking decisive action in the Spanish civil war. It is now quite clear that Franco's victory was the first, and may have been the decisive, defeat of the democracies in the second World War.

No leadership, no matter how courageous, can completely overcome the weakness of democracy in the realm of foreign policy. Its inability to act with the same foresight and ruthlessness as the tyrannical nations is one of those hazards which must be taken into account. The fact is this weakness would not have proved so nearly fatal (or really fatal) if the inevitable blindness of democracy in foreign policy had not been aggravated by a culture which increased this blindness. The common people are no fools. In fact they react with a wholesome common sense to the problems of the day. The fools were the intellectual leaders of our democracy who talked utopian nonsense in a critical decade in which the whole of western civilization faced its hour of doom. They confused the natural and wholesome political instincts of common folk until they were unable to recognize a terrible peril before the peril had become so immediate and imminent that weapons of defense had to be improvised.

In recent months many college faculties have been petitioning the President and Congress to send aid to the Allies as the best method of defending American vital interests and of preserving western civilization. The students of the universities have, on the whole, failed to follow the lead of their tutors and have persisted in a wholly unrealistic policy of isolation. They have insisted upon abiding by the previous counsels of their elders after the latter were forced to abandon them under the pressure of the hour. Nothing could prove more conclusively how inadequate

72

the whole temper of "liberalism" in our colleges has been. It has not prepared the young people to face the realities of our day. It has made utopian demands upon life and has resulted in cynical reactions because history failed to conform to these demands. In Dostoievsky's novel *The Possessed*, a father who lives in a world of utopian illusions prompts his son to a consistent and corrosive cynicism. The son realizes that nothing in life conforms to his father's dreams and therefore comes to the conclusion that nothing in life is worth while. The spiritual situation in our universities is strikingly analogous to the spiritual confusion of the intelligentsia of Russia in. Dostoievsky's day.

The elders have sufficient knowledge of immediate realities to be able and willing to renounce their unrealistic creeds in an hour of crisis in which they have become irrelevant. But the poor victims of their education have been so thoroughly indoctrinated with these creeds that they are unable to measure the perils in which they stand.

73

5

IDEALISTS AS CYNICS

No NATION HAS EVER been driven to political confusion in its judgments on foreign affairs by a greater variety of absolutist creeds than our contemporary America. The creeds are various, but they have in common the tendency to measure political realities, not in terms of possible historical alternatives, but by comparison with purely ideal possibilities. This is a fatal weakness in the realm of politics, for political values are highly relative. We never have the chance to choose between pure tyranny and pure freedom; we can only choose between tyranny and relative democracy. We do not have the choice between war and perfect peace, but only between war and the uneasy peace of some fairly decent and stable equilibrium of social forces. We cannot choose between violence and non-violence, but only between violence and a statesmanship which seeks to adjust social forces without violence but cannot guarantee immunity from clashes. We have never had the opportunity—and probably never shall have—to choose between injustice and perfect equality, but only between injustice and a justice which moves toward equality and incorporates some of its values.

This obvious fact, to which all history attests, is denied either explicitly or implicitly by a wide variety of modern social creeds. These creeds, each of which probably has its own validity within measure, have combined their errors in such a way as to spread confusion. They have created an attitude of irresponsibility toward the tragic history of Europe and a spirit of cynicism in estimating the consequences of the war.

The pacifists and the Socialists are one in believing that nothing is at stake in the present European struggle. The Socialists take this position because they measure the evils of a capitalist society against the ideal possibilities of a socialist commonwealth of nations. The pacifists measure them against an ideal world in which there will be neither coercion nor resistance. The Communists and the national patriots make confusion worse confounded by insisting that these ideal possibilities actually have been realized in some nations. The Communists are certain that Russia cannot be imperialistic or prompted by nationalist motives; they believe that only capitalist nations can be imperialistic. This conclusion might give pause to the Socialists, who also believe that only capitalist nations are, or can be, imperialistic but who condemn Russia. Stalin may have corrupted the universalist ideal of socialism more than necessary; but history is bound to insinuate partial loyalties into universal ideals. The national patriots differ from the Communists only in their belief that it is America rather than Russia which is free of the egotism and imperialism they condemn in other nations. In either its communist or its American form the belief that one is free of the vices one sees in others is a comforting faith and betrays a self-righteousness as old as history.

Pacifism is usually the creed of only a small minority in any nation. It has achieved more than minority proportions in contemporary America largely because our churches are almost unanimous in their espousal of it. They have been driven to this position by their uneasy conscience over their hysteria in the last war. They have not been spiritually and morally profound enough to see that abstaining from all judgment between the contending forces is not the only possible alternative to proclaiming a "holy war."

Pacifism is all the more popular in the churches because it is unconsciously mixed with the national fear of being involved in the war. In their anxiety to prove that they have purged themselves of the

77

uncritical hysteria to which they yielded in the last war, the churches are inclined to identify religious perfectionism with the morally dubious impulses of an irresponsible nationalism. Religious perfectionism in ascetic terms probably has a greater validity than modern men realize. It may be a wholesome protest against all political relativities. But when a religious and moral absolute such as "perfect love" is introduced into politics as an alternative to the contest of power which is the very nature of politics, it breeds confusion. One form that this confusion takes is the disinclination of the pacifists to look at the horrible consequences of tyranny lest they be shaken in their conviction that nothing can possibly be worse than war.

The Socialists are inclined to cynical detachment from this war because they are secure in their conviction that war is the inevitable consequence of the capitalist economy. The genuine differences between Nazi tyranny and the cultural and social virtues of what is still left of civilization in Europe are thus obscured. It is of course important to be extremely critical of the motives and actions of the oligarchs who control modern democratic society. It is also well to remember that Hitler could not imperil all of Europe today if it were not for the treason of those oligarchs to the cause of democracy yesterday. It is also important to strive for a new organization of our economic life so that the capitalistic decay undermining the whole of western civilization will not aggravate the anarchy of nations.

But it is hardly realistic to assume that a "new" society will automatically be free of national egotisms and rivalries, or even that the problem of preventing the "rulers" of a new society from becoming traitors to the essential interests of their commonwealths is permanently solved. Utopianism is always a source of confusion in dealing with immediate issues, because it accentuates the evils encountered by comparing them with perfections which history does not know and probably will never know. Many contemporary utopians, for instance, believe that a long-drawn-out war issuing in a stalemate would be a good thing because it would produce a general breakdown, in which the British tories and French reactionaries would be swept out before a socialist revolution. It is of course more probable that such a breakdown would bring, not socialism, but the totalitarianism from which Germany now suffers. If recent history has taught us anything it is that social organisms do not entertain with equanimity the prospect of a breakdown, from which a new society is to emerge. Rather they seek to ward it off by reconstructions of their disintegrated economy under dictatorships. History ought therefore to have discounted social catastrophism as a political philosophy. Yet we find radicals

79

who were once rigorous "social democrats" turning to catastrophism.

When utopian illusions are dispelled and one is not so certain what lies on the other side of social breakdown, either in terms of ideal possibilities or actual historical alternatives, one does not lightly hope for the breakdown of any social system in which there is still a degree of freedom and the possibility of achieving better social and economic adjustments. One hopes for such a breakdown only when any alternative is preferable to the existing tyranny.

The Communists, who still have a remarkably large following among intellectuals, add to the confusion of socialist utopianism by clinging to the absurd belief that utopia is in some measure a reality in Russia. This forces them to condone imperialist and nationalist motives in Russian politics which they profess to abhor in the capitalist nations, and to measure every political development by its effect upon Russian success. Thus they united with the pacifists in deprecating American sympathy for Finland.

In this welter of conflicting dogmas it may be difficult to remember what ought not to be forgotten: that the anarchy of western civilization has produced a particularly virulent form of tyranny in Europe; that this tyranny has destroyed every authentic form of culture in Germany and threatens every liberty in Europe; that the destruction of this tyranny, while only a negative condition of new health, is nevertheless a very .important one. The fall of the Nazis would not of course of itself create a new Germany or a new Europe. Whether another vindictive and abortive peace shall be made or whether Europe can lift the whole problem of security to a new level of international interdependence, is the paramount issue before western society. A vindictive peace would mean that this war would be merely a milestone in the tragic course of European civilization toward ultimate disintegration.

Undoubtedly this issue will be fought out in the democratic nations on class lines, and the labor forces will have to make the largest contributions to a creative peace. But forces of sanity transcending class lines are engaged in the struggle. We may have reached a point in history in which the fear of alternatives too terrible to face will drive the usually stupid nations to seek security on a new level of creativeness. The fear of death, we are told, is an element in the travails of birth and furnishes some of the energy which makes birth possible. It is at any rate highly irresponsible to take a purely cynical attitude toward the possibilities of a decent peace. "If hopes are dupes, fears may be liars." Such an attitude is particularly blame-

worthy here because assumption of a responsible relation to this problem by America may well become
a decisive factor in the peace.

However speculative the outcome of this tragic
struggle may be, the attitude of cynicism, prompted
by a disappointed idealism, is morally intolerable.
That is a lesson which our present generation of college students has yet to learn. They are now pretty
generally engaged in proving that since all war
news is propaganda they are absolved of the responsibility of seeking for the truth amid conflicting
claims. In this they merely reflect the prevailing mood
of their elders. America has contrived to brew self-
righteousness, cynicism, idealism, and a fear psychosis
into a pretty horrible mixture.

6

PEACE AND THE LIBERAL ILLUSION*

THE CAPITULATION OF Munich was obviously caused in part by the fact that the oligarchy which holds the strategic positions in our capitalistic democracies does not really intend to protect democracy against fascism if such a defense would lead to the destruction of fascism and a consequent social revolution. On the other hand, the tory oligarchs, for whom Chamberlain, Daladier, and Bonnet were the typical spokesmen, could not have succeeded in an essentially treasonable policy if a healthy spirit of opposition to their program had not been enervated among the general populace by political and moral confusion. These confusions, which are, broadly speaking, liberal confusions, have their source

*First published, January 28, 1939.

in the basic cultural presuppositions underlying democratic life. The crisis of Munich therefore raised the question whether democracy as a political technique has an adequate cultural foundation for meeting the challenge of fascism.

The cultural foundation of fascism is Nietzschean romanticism, with its glorification of force and vitality as self-justifying, combined with primitive romanticism, with its substitution of racial and tribal particularism for liberal universalism. The cultural foundation of western democracy is eighteenth- and nineteenth-century liberalism. This liberalism rests upon rationalistic optimism. It believes that it is comparatively easy to "substitute reason for force" and that mankind is embarked on a progressive development which will substitute "free co-operative inquiry" for political partisanship and social conflict. It regards the peculiar ambitions and desires of races and nations as irrationalities which must gradually yield to universal values, generally recognized and established by reason, that is, by some kind of discarnate reason of pure objectivity. Democracy, in other words, rests upon a faith in the essential goodness of man and the possibility of completely rational behavior.

Is it possible to meet the challenge of a civilization which glorifies force if the relation of force to reason in political action is understood no better than liberalism understands it? Is it possible to maintain any degree of universalism against tribal fanaticism and particularism if the relation of the organic unities of race and nation to a civilization which transcends them is not comprehended in more dialectical terms than it is by liberalism? Is it possible to resist a civilization organized for war if the forces which seek to guide mankind to a pacific way of life do not understand that political tension and friction between contending political wills are normal, or at least inevitable, characteristics of national and international life? Is liberalism, in short, not too simple a creed to suit the complexities of our tragic era?

It would be sad indeed if democracy in political life were to succumb to fascism because the liberalism which supports it creates confusion in critical hours. For democracy in politics is a perennial necessity; and liberalism may prove to be no more than a passing middle-class illusion in a brief period of expanding capitalism. Democracy is a perennial necessity because justice will always require that the power of government be checked as democracy checks it; and because peace requires that social conflict be arbitrated by the non-violent technique of the democratic process.

Democracy as a political system is important precisely because liberalism as a culture is not based on truth, that is, because its interpretation of human nature is fallacious and too optimistic. Power must be held under democratic restraints because irresponsible power is always dangerous. It is dangerous because a dominant oligarchy always pretends a false identity between its interests and the general welfare. Methods of arbitrating conflicting social interests must be found precisely because various social groups cannot be expected to have perfect, rational conformity of interests. A non-violent expression of the claims and counter-claims of politics is important precisely because political arguments are never merely rational arguments. The threat of force against recalcitrant minorities is always implied in them. If this is not understood, the liberal is in danger of betraying the essentials of a democratic civilization for the sake of loyalty to democratic principles, that is, for the principle of arbitration with the foe. If the foe happens to represent a civilization which incarnates war as the ultimate good, the liberal may sacrifice the institutions of peace for the sake of a peaceful settlement with a foe who intends to destroy them. Thus peace is lost for peace's sake, because it is not understood that there are moments in history when the covert threat of force which underlies all political contention must be brought into the open. If it is brought into the open by a foe who may be weaker than you but who glories in the threat and pretends to desire overt conflict, he will have the advantage of you despite your greater strength. If you have given publicity to your moral scruples and your political confusion, he will have the greater advantage. He will make impossible demands because he knows that you have been foolish enough to draw an absolute moral distinction between the threat of force which underlies all political conflict and the overt use of force into which it will occasionally develop.

It is necessary to repeat that we do not accuse Chamberlain and Daladier of having worked under the disadvantages of such scruples. But it is apparent that they could be celebrated as apostles of peace and of the "Christian method" only because such confusion existed. Throughout the crisis *The London Times,* for instance, accepted the dismemberment of Czecho-Slovakia with equanimity. Indeed, it suggested the idea of such a settlement at a time when the governments were not ready for it. But it insisted that Hitler would have to enter Czecho-Slovakia in a gentlemanly and decent fashion. "To the nations of the free western tradition," it declared, "no solution is tolerable except the way of reason." By this it meant nothing but a demand that the victor hide the nakedness of his sword as he brandished it over the vanquished. Hitler must enter the prostrate democracy according to a timetable. Political realities, such as the shift of power which would result from the dismemberment of the unhappy nation, were obscured.

The Times called for a "judgment upon the plain

merits and demerits of the German demands" and
insisted that this judgment, to be "utterly realistic,"
must exclude "speculative opinions whether Herr
Hitler can be made to yield without fighting and
whether his regime can face the strain of a war."
The Times, in other words, believed, or pretended to
believe for the sake of its moralistic readers, that
there is a transcendent perspective in politics, fortunately located in Britain, where the "plain merits
and demerits" of the case could be judged; and it
also pretended to believe that the assessment of German strength and weakness which occupied every
chancellery of Europe was an irrelevance. *The
Times* hailed the peace of Munich as a triumph of
"reason over force." It grudgingly recognized that this
political argument was not an exercise in pure persuasion. "The gathering urgency of persuasion," it
admitted, "was reinforced with unmistakable proofs
of resolution for defense"; but fearful lest this ad-
mission of the horrors of politics might spoil the
picture of triumphant reason, it hastened to add,
"These things were not a threat, nor is it to be supposed that the German Chancellor would yield to
threats; but there is no doubt that the evidence that
Mr. Chamberlain offered concessions from strength
and not from weakness won him respect that might
not otherwise have been accorded."

It would be unfair to regard *The Times* as a typical

spokesman of the liberal creed. Its blandness is too perfect to be honest; and its function as voice of the British aristocracy suggests that it was consciously hiding the political realities of Munich rather than unconsciously obscuring them. But the letters which poured into its correspondence columns prove that among its readers were many who honestly believed that Munich represented a triumph of the methods of peace, of democracy, of civilization over the threat of war. Meanwhile Czecho-Slovakia lay prostrate under the heel of the conqueror, and a few days after Munich, Hitler spoke at Saarbrücken and thumbed his nose at the democracies who were supposed to have won his respect because they made concessions from strength and not from weakness.

The liberal culture which is unable to assess the relation of force to reason, to understand the coercive element in all political life, and to appreciate the "ideological" taint in all human reason when the interests of the reasoner are involved is compounded of the characteristic prejudices of academics and businessmen. In this compound is usually an admixture of denatured Christian perfectionism. This religious perfectionism has reduced Christian pacifism, which in its pure form knows martyrdom to be its end, to a counsel of prudence. It promises that the way of non-violence will in the long run gain a more certain victory over your foe than the way of violence; but

89

it is indefinite about the length of the run. This kind of Christianity prompted the Archbishop of Canterbury to hail the victory of Hitler in Austria because it was "bloodless."

To the culture of liberalism eighteenth- and nineteenth-century academics—and many belated colleagues in the twentieth century—contributed the idea of an increasingly discarnate rationality which would finally rise above the welter of human conflict and decide all contentious issues according to the "plain merits and demerits" of the case. The businessmen contributed to the illusions of liberalism for two reasons. For one thing they were the first oligarchs who held their dominant position in society by the exercise of covert, or economic, rather than overt, or military, power. As Bertrand Russell has recently observed, economic power does not kill but merely starves to death. Thus it meets the Archbishop of Canterbury's test of bloodlessness. Secondly, in the last two hundred years the wealth of the industrial nations increased and their political influence expanded so greatly that the realities of social conflict were obscured until the decay and contraction of this latter day set in.

For the same reason the illusions of liberalism are more stubborn in America than in any other country. The wealth of this nation and its geographic isolation have contributed to illusions which prompt our statesmen to lecture Europe on the advantages of "reason over force" while building a larger navy.

There are those who insist that Marxism has added to the confusion created by liberalism and who even believe that Marxist parties helped to enervate the resolution of the democratic nations in their recent hour of trial. This charge must be refuted, at least in part. The inadequacy of a man like Léon Blum in the crisis obviously stems from his liberalism rather than from his Marxism. Marxism has in fact been denatured to a considerable degree by liberalism in all western democratic nations. The fact is that Marxism, in its pure form, has been the most potent critic of liberal illusions. Who understands the pretensions of "rational objectivity" in social conflict better than a real Marxist? Or for that matter the invalidity of an absolute distinction between the covert and the overt use of force? Yet the provisional realism of the Marxists quickly results in new illusions and confusions. Since capitalism is regarded as the root of all injustice—rather than as what it is in fact, the most potent source of ecenomic injustice in contemporary society—the Communist Marxist inclines to regard Russian diplomacy as, by definition, a force of pure disinterestedness in international affairs and to dismiss charges of political injustice in Russia with incredulity. The Socialist Marxist, on the other hand, seeking to take position of uncompromising opposition to capitalism vacated by the Communist opportunists, insists that since all evil comes, by definition, from capitalism, it is an error to make any distinction between British imperialism and German fascism. Thus he makes common cause with the liberal who will not defend democracy because it would cease to be democracy if he defended it. The Socialist will not defend democracy because it is not pure democracy but is corrupted with capitalistic injustice.

If to the liberal illusions of the middle classes and the simplicity of Marxist judgments we add the dishonesties of the capitalistic oligarchs who prefer fascism to an extension of democracy, we have a cultural situation which, if not corrected, is bound to lead to the complete triumph of fascism. It is certainly the principal explanation for the fateful tardiness of democratic civilization in resisting fascist aggression up to the present time.

Nietzschean morality perversely transposes all values and raises the disease of social life, conflict, to the eminence of the criterion of all values. If it is to be defeated, the civilization which defeats it must be informed by a culture which understands that, though disease is not normal, its perils are constant, and that some of the best medicines are poisons taken in moderation. A liberal culture does not understand man in the unity of his body and soul, in the urgency of his physical needs, in the interestedness of all rational processes when they are concerned with his vital wants. It does not understand, therefore, the necessity of coercion for the sake of securing social co-operation and the necessity of resistance to power for the sake of securing justice. It habitually hides its covert brutalities from its own conscience and sickens at the thought of protecting what is still valuable and genuine in its culture from the overt brutalities of a resolute foe.

It may be that democracy is too intimately bound up with these liberal prejudices to survive their destruction. This is a pity. For if democracy dies it must be born again. There is no way to justice without it.

7

GREEK TRAGEDY AND MODERN POLITICS*

O<small>NE OF THE RECURRING</small> motifs of Greek tragedy is the hero's deeper involvement in his fate through his very efforts to extricate himself from it. Thus in the Œdipus cycle the father of Œdipus is warned that his son will kill him. To avert this fate he exposes the new-born infant to the weather, but the boy is rescued by a kindly shepherd, and is brought to maturity by a foster-father, whom he regards as his real father. Fearful of becoming guilty of his supposed father's death, the youth flees from home, only to come into deadly encounter with his real father on the way. In the same manner the sons of Œdipus seek to avoid the curse which their father has pronounced upon them by ruling their

*First published, January 1, 1938.

kingdom alternately, a policy which leads to civil war and the very consequence of mutual destruction which they sought to avoid.

The modern international situation offers abundant proof of the profound insight into human tragedy of the Greek dramatists. They were not writing melodrama but were interpreting history, including that of modern times. The history of our era seems to move in tragic circles, strangely analogous to those presented symbolically in Greek tragedy. The democratic nations of the world are involving themselves more inexorably in world catastrophe by their very efforts to avert or to avoid it.

The political tension of the modern world is created by the aggressive attitude of the so-called have-not nations, the hungry powers, which happen also to be the fascist powers. The defenders of the status quo are the more or less satisfied nations, which happen also to be the protagonists of democracy.

History does not justify simple moral judgments. To regard the democratic nations as "good" because they are seeking to preserve peace does not mean that we can hold them guiltless in their relation to the whole chain of vicious circles which constitute recent history. The fury of the hungry nations is partly the evil fruit of the vindictiveness of the victorious nations. The fact that the defenders of the status quo are also the defenders of democracy reveals the ambiguous character of the struggle. Nevertheless, we may forget the past for the moment and record only the obvious fact that the fascist powers, chiefly Japan, Germany, and Italy, have forms of government which can exist only by threat and aggression. Their whole economy is subordinated to their military objectives and can justify itself only if it can achieve imperial aims commensurate with their desperate martial preparations.

Yet none of these nations wanted a major war. All were too poor to bear the burden of a long conflict. What they wanted was to be left alone by the powerful nations while they devoured lesser nations in their vicinity. Thus Japan is at war with China. But it is a war into which it would not have dared if it had not known that the democratic powers would not interfere.

The economic weakness of the fascist powers determines their diplomacy. They bluff the dominant powers into acquiescence to their still minor military exploits by threatening to involve the world in war if their objectives are not granted. They can afford to engage in these bluffs because they do not have to consider the public fear of war which places a check upon the maneuvers of statesmen in democratic nations. It is, for instance, a fairly well-established fact that when Germany militarized the Rhineland it averted French and English intervention by threatening to retaliate with a terrible aerial bombardment. Germany knew very well at that time that it was not prepared for a war against France and England. But an after-us-the-deluge recklessness proved to be a successful type of diplomacy. It is, in fact, this "gangster" diplomacy which has obtained one diplomatic triumph after another for the fascist nations. It would of course be naïve to distinguish this type of diplomacy too sharply from that traditionally engaged in by all the nations, for diplomacy has never lacked this element of bluff. Nevertheless, governments less obviously constructed for a desperate hour and with some sense of responsibility for the future, whether they be democratic or monarchial, are embarrassed by inhibitions which the new dictatorships lack completely.

Britain has sought to dissuade Germany from aggression on the continent by offering her various minor compensations. But the one thing Britain would not do was to give a wholly unambiguous undertaking to France, in the event of German aggression. The uncertainty thus created is not as great as that which contributed to the outbreak of hostilities in 1914, but it is very similar and must have similar consequences. By seeking to reserve a decision which historical destiny has made inevitable (namely the decision to support France in the final extremity), the fate of ultimate conflict, which she seeks to avoid by this indecision, is thus made more unavoidable.

Just as Britain tries to make herself believe that she does not belong to the continent and can escape responsibility for it, we try to make ourselves believe that we do not belong to the same world with Europe. Our attitude in this respect must have the same consequence of accentuating by our irresponsibility the anarchy of nations which must ultimately become wide enough to engulf us, precisely because we helped to widen it. The tragic circle must thus be completed for both Britain and America.

Why are the democratic nations so tragically committed to this dance of death? One answer is that the democratic nations are also the great capitalistic nations. Their economic power, which alone would be sufficient, if artfully applied, to stop the fascist ventures, is not wholly on the side of democracy, or even wholly on the side of the imperial interests of these nations. A social war happens to cross the international conflict just as it did in the days when Athens and Sparta fought for the hegemony of Greece. The dominant financial groups in the democratic nations are afraid that a too vigorous stand against the fascist powers will lead to the spread of communism. At the same time the mystery surrounding Russia and the

99

fear that its perpetual purges indicate some serious loss of inner cohesion and morale have contributed to France's undue dependence upon Britain.

Class interests tend to create centers of sympathy for fascism in every democratic nation. Since democracy is a potential peril to every privileged class, this is not altogether surprising. But it is strange that the dominant economic groups should be such poor defenders of their imperial interests. In Britain Winston Churchill upbraided the government in the closing days of the last Parliament for allowing Franco to mount guns levelled at Gibraltar; and Lloyd George inquired, in the opening days of the new Parliament, whether Spanish guns on the coast were not a menace to British ships in the Mediterranean. When the ministry answered that the ships could be protected by smoke screens, Lloyd George taunted the government for leaning upon so slender a reed. "We have become," said a leader of the Labor Party facetiously, "the champions of empire against the Tories." These incidents reveal to what degree the interests of a ruling class have become incompatible with the total interests of the empire which it built and upon which it must rely for its continuance.

Perhaps this incompatibility spells the doom of the British Empire. For, while the interests of a ruling oligarchy are never wholly compatible with the total interests of the nation or empire, complete incompatibility is an omen of decay and death. It is this contradiction between imperial interests and Tory class interests which makes explicable the duplicity and deviousness of British policy in regard to Spain. Britain did not want the Loyalists to win because its capitalistic interests would suffer if Spain had a radical government; it did not want Franco to win because Italian imperialism would thereby be fastened on the Iberian Peninsula. Hence the British Foreign Office equivocated with endless nonintervention proposals, each more transparently dishonest than the last.

It would be erroneous, however, to attribute the ineptitude of the democratic powers wholly to the influence of the capitalistic groups within these nations. Democracy itself is at a disadvantage in dealing with dictators. It is not easy to convince the general public that the risk involved in calling the bluff of the dictators is a justified risk. The general electorate can hardly be expected to have a clear understanding of the nation's fateful involvement in the total world problem. In America, for instance, any scheme of collective security is probably opposed more vigorously by a Middle Western farmer than by an Eastern banker.

The general public not only does not see the total picture which alone can justify the risks democratic nations must take, but gives itself to moralistic ·illusions about the nature of politics. It fondly hopes that generosity toward dictators will assuage their appetites, instead of merely giving them occasion for regarding "liberal" democracy as a craven and corrupt form of government which they have a mission to destroy. The saintly George Lansbury, erstwhile leader of the British Labor Party, is the perfect symbol of this moral hope. He thinks that he can dissolve the dynamics of fascism by personal conferences with Hitler and Mussolini.

Since politics in general and international politics in particular spell a contest of power in which moral arguments alone have never dissuaded a nation from a desired course of action, this simple moralism of the democratic peoples represents a rather naïve application of principles drawn from the observation of individual behavior to the problem of collective behavior. This is a natural error of individuals who have made no careful study of and have no direct contact with the problems of statecraft. In the present moment it serves some of the ruling oligarchies very well. During the Italian-Ethiopian crisis the do-nothing policy of the Tories was admirably supported by the pacifist hopes of labor and the Church people. Thus an illusion of the democratic classes serves to accentuate the equivocation of the plutocratic classes in our modern democracies.

In one sense the simple moralism of the democratic

nations is not so much the illusion of untutored individuals as the error of a whole system. All the democratic nations are informed by cultural presuppositions which had their rise in eighteenth-century rationalism. This rationalism attributes human wrongdoing to ignorance and holds to the implicit or explicit hope that a general advance of human knowledge will eliminate human conflict by "inculcating in all men the same principles of virtue and goodness," to quote Auguste Comte, the philosopher of positivism. This whole culture analyzes the facts of human nature falsely and fails to understand the organic relation between reason and passion or reason and interest. Its mistakes are particularly apparent in its analysis of collective behavior, but it is equally mistaken in its estimate of individuals. The fact is that even individuals are more persistently egotistic and use their cultural and spiritual achievements as instruments of egotism more generally than the culture of modernity realizes.

It is significant that the fascist nations have broken with this "liberal" culture as completely as they have rejected democratic politics. Broadly speaking, they follow Nietzsche's romantic glorification of power as self-justifying. Having disavowed the nation's responsibility for any so-called "universal" values, they feel able to destroy the last vestiges of a universal European culture without a qualm of conscience.

Their unqualified rejection of universal values in history leads to a cruel nihilism, just as the too simple moralism, rationalism, and universalism of the "liberal" nations lead them into hypocrisy in assessing their own actions and ambitions, and to false hopes when they estimate the probable actions of their opponents.

History would add a cruel irony to the tragedy of the self-destruction of modern democracies if it developed that what is still left of a universal culture and an ordered civilization could not protect itself against moral nihilism and political anarchy because a liberal civilization had assessed the weight of morality in politics too highly. All political justice is achieved by coercing the anarchy of collective self-interest into some kind of decent order by the most attainable balance of power. Such a balance, once achieved, can be stabilized, embellished, and even, on occasion, perfected by more purely moral considerations. But there has never been a scheme of justice in history which did not have a balance of power at its foundation. If the democratic nations fail, their failure must be partly attributed to the faulty strategy of idealists who have too many illusions when they face realists who have too little conscience. The false strategy will not be derived purely from the illusions of the idealists about their foes but from their illusions about themselves.

The democracies may still have enough power to win a war in which they are involving themselves by trying to avoid it. But they certainly will make the catastrophe of war more inevitable by their effort to escape it.

8

IDEOLOGY AND PRETENSE*

Ｉｎ ａｎａｌｙｚｉｎｇ ｔｈｅ Ｒｕｓｓｉａｎ or any other political situation a simple cynicism is no more illuminating than a simple moralism. To condone recent Russian politics on the ground that it is merely "power politics" in a world in which the power game is still being played and in which defensive necessities require participation in the game, counters the criticism of only those moral purists who are under the illusion that politics can be sublimated into an exercise of pure moral suasion. Every one else knows that all political struggles are power-political struggles, in the sense that contending forces avail themselves not only of rational and moral arguments but of whatever social power they control.

The real issue does not lie in the use of power, but

*First published, December 9, 1939.

in the relation of national interests to the universal values which transcend a nation. Every national organism seeks to defend itself, and possibly to extend its power and prestige, in competition with other nations. Every nation claims that in doing this it is fighting not only for its own existence but for certain values which transcend its existence. This claim need not be wholly spurious. It cannot be wholly spurious, in fact, if it is to achieve any degree of plausibility. But the claim is always more unqualified than the facts warrant. Thus Germany claimed, until recently, that it was fighting not only for its own existence but to preserve the world from bolshevism. Britain and France claimed they were fighting for democracy, but that did not prevent them from scuttling the democratic cause in Spain. America was even more intent upon the defeat of fascism than were France or Russia; but we were prevented from going to war against a fascist nation by the fact that our vital interests were not immediately imperiled by fascist aggression. Russia was at the center of the whole united-front movement against fascism until it appeared that the defensive requirements of the Russian state were better served by an alliance with, rather than against, Germany.

These States are all in the same position—their devotion to the cause or interest which transcends their national interest is not so complete as they pretend it to be. No nation is ever true to the cause which transcends its national life if there is not some coincidence between the defensive necessities of that cause and the defensive requirements of the national organism. Every nation pretends, on the other hand, that its primary loyalty is to a universal value. This is the element of deceit which is involved in all national life, and in all human existence for that matter; for individuals, as well as nations, sanctify partial and particular interests by identifying them unduly with universal values. Why they should do this has never been adequately analyzed in Marxist theory, though Marxism undoubtedly made a tremendous contribution to the discovery of the fact.

Whether we judge this or that nation more or less severely for engaging in these pretenses depends upon our own ideological bias. Thus the same comrades who tore their hair over Chamberlain's disloyalty to democracy through his policy of appeasement are quite complacent toward Stalin's pact with Hitler, though the latter obviously freed Germany to make its attack on Poland and to plunge Europe into war. In domestic politics all of us, whether of the right or the left, are similarly influenced. If our cause is supported by Constitution and tradition, we claim that our primary concern is the preservation of constitutional government. If constitutional procedure favors the enemy, we convince ourselves that nothing is so important as to challenge tradition.

The recognition of this universal ideological taint in human affairs, including the inclination to be conscious of the foe's dishonesty but not of our own, does not, however, do full justice to the problem involved in the Nazi Soviet Pact. Russia is a slightly different case, being the national embodiment of an international movement which claims to have risen above nationalism and imperialism in politics and above "ideology" (in the exact sense of that word) in culture. It is the thesis of Marxism that rationalization of interest is characteristic of bourgeois society but that a classless society is free of this dishonesty. It is the Marxist claim that nationalism is a product of capitalism and that the sentiment of nationality is transcended in the new society. Marxist doctrine affirms that the state is merely the instrument of class domination, that power and coercion are necessary only so long as the classless society is forced to contend against internal and external foes. When these are defeated the State will wither away.

The proof that these claims are taken seriously is given by the fact that thousands, if not millions, of the faithful outside the boundaries of Russia are completely devoted to its cause because they regard it not as a nation among other nations but as primarily a force of proletarian revolution in the world. Their devotion is so complete that their loyalty remains unshaken even when all the evidence points to the fact that the defensive, and possibly the imperialistic, requirements of the Russian State, rather than the strategic considerations of the workers' cause, determine Russian policy. They remain devoted even when *Izvestia* disavows the whole "ideological" battle line of yesterday and declares that like or dislike of fascism is a matter of taste.

The problem which this situation presents to the progressive and labor forces of the world cannot be dismissed by the cynical reminder that Russia is merely a nation like every other nation and like every other must play the game of power politics. If this is all that Russia is, it does not deserve the devotion of the nationals of other countries, and one can hardly blame other nations for seeking to destroy or to suppress the primary allegiance of some of its citizens to a "foreign state"; for this loyalty gives Russia an undue advantage in the game of power politics.

Obviously Russia is still in some measure loyal to a proletarian civilization which transcends its national existence. Yet it is bound to interpret this international cause in terms which practically identify it with Russian national interests. This ambiguity of

Russian politics will become an increasing source of peril to the radical cause in other nations.

If this problem is probed to its full depth, it may appear not only that the Stalinist interpretation of Marxism will have to be challenged but that the Marxist theory of ideology will have to be reexamined. Whatever its great merits in uncovering the relation of economic interest to moral, legal, and cultural ideas and ideals, Marxist theory has become a source of moral and political confusion by attributing ideology to economic class interest alone, when as a matter of fact the ideological taint is a permanent factor of human culture on every level of advance.

The fact is that the most potent form of pretension arises at the very point in culture where the claim is made that all partial perspectives have been transcended, and where it is assumed that a political force in conflict with other forces is in fact a transcendental force, moving above the welter of interest and passion. Modern culture confronts in modern communism exactly the same problem which the Reformation and the Renaissance faced in Catholicism at the dawn of the modern age. The Catholic Church claimed to be, not a particular religious, political, and cultural force imbedded in the feudal order and sanctifying particular political interests, but an absolute and transcendental force. It is because the claim of ultimate and absolute validity is always involved in religion that Marx rightly declared, "The beginning of all criticism is the criticism of religion." That truth must now be applied to Marxism itself insofar as it is not merely a political movement dealing with particular abuses but a religious movement claiming to have a solution for the ultimate problems of human existence. Catholics and Communists are both bound to resent this comparison, but that does not prove it to be untrue. Rival absolutists are not likely to recognize affinities in their conflicting ultimate claims, for they are too impressed by the difference in content to note the similarity in method.

The ideological taint, the dishonest pretension of universality, which accompanies every partial perspective in history does not mean that significant choices between rival political movements cannot be made; we are still capable of making them, though we are ourselves involved in rationalization and have no absolute and impartial perspective. If there were not some degree of freedom from interest in the human mind, there could be no culture at all, and all life would be no more than a conflict of interests. But our choices will be less confused if we know how to discount the latest ideology, which always presents itself in the guise of a final freedom from rationalization. It was important for Renaissance rationalists to discount the claim of a feudal civilization that it was a final form of civilization because it was "Christian." It was equally important for the Marxist to discover that the "objective" and "impartial" social scientists of the liberal-bourgeois period subtly insinuated bourgeois perspectives into their objective scientific conclusions.

The contemporary task is to unmask the rationalizations of these same Marxists, who wrongly assume that the class organization of society is the sole source of ideological pretension. The pretensions of Russia must be judged as those of any other nation. Its transcendent disinterestedness in the field of world politics is an illusion. A proletarian civilization cannot be assumed to be good merely because it is proletarian. That a dictatorship which worships power for its own sake and another which rests upon the utopian illusion that all power can be eliminated from human life should reveal so many striking similarities is a perfect revelation of the moral and political confusion of our era.

The similarity between the dictatorships has now been extended to the field of propaganda. The Russians professed themselves imperiled by the aggression of the Finns, just as the Germans pictured themselves the long-suffering victims of Polish aggression, and acted accordingly. Thus Russia has graduated into the position of a completely modern State. Not only does it engage in the general rationalizations of which all nations avail themselves and which consist in interpreting facts from a particular national perspective, but it has learned the art of the tyrannical State, which so controls all organs of opinion that it can manufacture, rather than merely interpret, facts to suit its purposes.

9

SYNTHETIC BARBARISM

THE CONFLICT BETWEEN the western democracies and the totalitarian powers repeats a perennial theme of history. Civilized communities have always had to face and have frequently succumbed to, the peril of barbarian invasion. The barbarians usually lacked the technical advantages of the civilized communities but their simpler social organization and their more primitive will-to-power frequently outweighed the technical advantages of civilization. Civilized communities were handicapped by both their virtues and their vices in meeting the barbarian threat. The weakness which is occasioned by the vices of civilization makes every such barbarian invasion seem to be a just retribution upon the sins of advanced societies. The weakness which is derived from civilized virtues gives a tragic note to history and makes it appear that some law of diminishing returns perennially destines civilization to destroy itself.

In the present international conflict this recurring theme of history is repeated with one important distinction. For the first* time in history the barbarians which threaten civilization have been generated in the heart of a decadent civilization. The barbarism which threatens us is "synthetic" rather than genuine. Its vitality is not primitive but primitivistic. It represents a romantic effort to hide and to heal a decadence deeper than the disease from which the western nations suffer. A barbarism developed in the heart of civilization has one important advantage over genuinely primitive barbarisms. It avails itself of all the technical advantages of civilization. Nazi barbarism may have destroyed the pure sciences but it uses the heritage of the applied sciences to full advantage. Germany has destroyed all high religion and all advanced philosophy, but its engineers have worked to better advantage in fashioning instruments of destruction than the engineers of civilization.

However, this synthetic barbarism also has one disadvantage in comparison with genuinely primitive barbarism. It has imposed a primitivistic will-to-

*Possibly for the second time. Sparta was also a synthetic barbarism.

power and a simple tribal social organization upon the complexities of a civilized community. It has substituted a decadent cynicism for the instinctive power impulses of barbarism. This makes for a cruelty more terrible than a genuinely primitive cruelty. But on the other hand it actually accentuates the social failure which it is intended to obscure and to heal. For this reason the pattern of the present social conflict is determined by the tremendous question whether this new barbarism can overwhelm civilization by its momentary advantages before its inherent weaknesses begin to manifest themselves. It was generally assumed that this was not possible. This assumption was so generally held in the civilized communities that it actually added to their complacency in meeting the threat of barbarism. Whether the assumption will be ultimately justified remains an open question of contemporary history.

The primitive community has an instinctive social cohesion, rooted in the force of consanguinity. Its cement of cohesion is furnished by nature and not by mind. This primitive unity and solidarity gives the barbaric tribe advantages over civilization, in which social complexity always threatens to dissolve the forces of social cohesion. The Germans have sought to restore this simple community of "blood" in a society in which social conflict had corroded the more complex unity which civilization at its best is able to achieve. They superimposed this unity upon the multifarious forms of life and culture in which civilization expresses itself. The price of such an achievement is tyranny and despotism in the field of politics and the destruction of culture in the realms of the spirit. No such tyranny can finally maintain itself amidst the complexities of civilized life. But there is a bare possibility that it can destroy civilization to such a degree that it will be able to preserve a tyrannical unity of a nation and even of a European empire, longer than any of us would like to believe.

II

Every civilized community tends to create and to suffer from an oligarchy which once performed a creative task in organizing the community. It tends to become increasingly burdensome in the period of decay when it exacts more wealth from the community than its services deserved or require and when it reveals instincts of survival as a special class which come in direct conflict with the defensive needs of the community as a whole. Thus Athens was at a disadvantage in its contest with the synthetic barbarism of Sparta because of the double-mindedness of its aristocracy. In the same fashion modern Britain and France were almost delivered into the hands of their enemies by their Tory and capitalistic oligarchies before they awoke belatedly to the peril

of this treason. The disinclination of the Tory oligarchy in Britain to take the most obvious precautions
against the threat to its empire in the Spanish Civil
War, because that war also imperilled Tory class interests, is symbolic of the peril to which a great
community becomes exposed when the interests of its
oligarchy stand in complete contradiction to the interests of the total community.

The significance of Winston Churchill lies in the
fact that his mind was always informed by a more
clear-sighted imperialistic will, in which class interests had not obscured the basic realities of the imperial struggle. That he should have come to power
in the final hour of crisis and should have been given
his opportunity by the refusal of Labor to serve under Chamberlain reveals the coincidence between the
survival impulses of a great imperial community and
the survival impulses of a democratic civilization,
which partially transcends and which is partially embodied in the imperial community. That he should
have come to power only in the final hour of crisis
is indicative of the degree of confusion in which a
civilized community may be plunged by the leadership of its oligarchy and from which only the direct
and most patent immediate peril rescues it.

In comparison the ruling oligarchies of the
totalitarian powers seem to have fewer divergent
interests from those of the total community. The

primitivistic tribalism which created them or which they created, has made an end of "economic man" and divergent economic interests. The oligarchy seems to be devoted with complete singleness of mind to the pride and prestige of their national community. Yet these totalitarian chiefs have little in common with primitive warrior chieftains, for all their pretended mystic identification with the nation. They are not authentic bearers of the nation's will or they would not have to maintain themselves by terror; nor would they have to seek to enhance the pride and prestige of the nation by a hazardous diplomacy and an even more hazardous warfare. Only dictators can indulge in a diplomacy which outrages all canons of caution and can prepare for wars upon the principle of "all or nothing." The instinctive caution of democratic communities, in which the fears and apprehensions of the common man help to determine national policy, places them at a tremendous disadvantage in a contest with these tyrannies.

It may be doubted, however, whether the tyrannies can maintain their advantage in the long run. Ultimately it will be revealed that the victories which a fascist oligarchy is able to achieve in both diplomacy and war are not in the interest of their respective communities, though they may flatter national pride for a moment. Their primary purpose is to keep the fascist tyrants in power and to satisfy their own pride. If the tyrannies should gain a complete momentary victory over the civilized communities it may of course require decades before the essential treason of the tyrannical oligarchies is discovered. The elation of victory of their national communities will be great enough to engulf all impulses of caution for the moment and to obscure the perils to which a reckless politics exposes even the strongest State. This is why it is hopeless to expect any tyrannies to be destroyed from within, so long as they gain victories. They have corrupted the intelligence of their subjects too thoroughly to allow any internal checks upon reckless power to function.

III

Civilized communities suffer from another great disadvantage in facing the threat of barbarism. Among them intellectual sophistication tends to destroy an understanding for the elements of power which underlie all social structures. The primitive community, on the other hand, has an instinctive understanding for the play of power, which may be obscured or submerged but which cannot be eliminated from political life. The internal order and peace of a community and its security and stability in the total community of nations is not maintained by power alone. Internal peace and justice are maintained only by a decent organization of the mutually dependent and partially conflicting vitalities of national life. External peace depends upon the same principle of organization. Yet the internal justice of a community is never so perfect and the accommodation of interests so complete that any society could dispense with the alloy of coercion in the amalgam of its social peace. Nor is it possible to secure the external peace of a community in the partial, and sometimes total, anarchy of nations, without balancing power against power in times of peace and without setting power against power in times of war.

Stable and civilized communities tend to forget this fact. Their pacifism is the fruit of contradictory elements in their life. It is partly the consequences of the sloth and the love of ease which grows up in communities which have enjoyed long periods of internal and external stability. Something of the pride of a gentleman, who believes that the wayfaring bully is bound finally to respect his superior worth, enters into it. It betrays something of the ethos of the bourgeois trader who is certain that he can always buy off his adversary as a last resort and who is convinced that there is no conflict of interest which cannot be resolved in some kind of a "bargain." Our own bourgeois civilization is particularly subject to such illusions. It was simply unable to envisage the possibility that a resolute foe might be intent upon its annihilation or enslavement. This civilized pacifism is partly the consequence of a cultured individualism which rightly resents the tyranny of the collective will and wrongly imagines that the individual can free himself completely from his organic relations to race and nation.

The noblest element in this pacifism is generated by a sensitive religious and intellectualistic minority, developed in every Christian civilization. This minority has a long memory and an uneasy conscience about the injustices which lie at the foundation of every national and imperial existence. It has some understanding for the fact that the judgment of God is directed against every civilization because of the injustices which corrupt its life. But in our own day, particularly, this religious insight has become corrupted by utopian illusions and our culture has given itself to the vain imagination that there is some simple alternative to the residual injustices of every scheme of justice. Our sensitive minority either imagines that justice would be served by handing a tainted civilization over to the barbarians or that the barbarians could be beguiled from their ferocity by a show of generosity. It hasn't the slightest understanding of the fact that a genuine barbarian, and even more a synthetic barbarian, may hold the virtues of humanity, which are intended to beguile him, in complete contempt.

The relation between the uneasy conscience of the

sensitive British minority and the complacency of the British oligarchy toward fascist aggregation is a subject which will intrigue future historians. Here virtue and vice are curiously mingled. In America the moral confusion is even worse than in Britain because our religious life has become so completely divorced from the classical Christian faith, with its profound understanding of the complexities and tragedies of history, and has become so completely enmeshed in the illusions of rationalistic utopianism, that most of our religious idealists are quite ready to submit to tryanny in the name of peace, to enthrone a system of perpetual war in western civilization in the interest of avoiding war, and to deliver a civilization of partial justice into the hands of a barbarism which denies the very concept of justice because they have an uneasy conscience about the injustice from which civilization has been unable to free itself.

The primitive community's instinctive understanding of the place of power in political life gives it real advantages over the advanced communities with their noble scruples and their ignoble delusions. But Germany can hardly be said to have this advantage. It has imposed the power impulse as a Nietzschian ideal upon the moral sensibilities of a once civilized people.

The decadent brutalities which are the fruit of this

development offer perils to civilization, greater than
any which proceeded from a more genuine barbarism.
But they also offer greater perils to the life of Germany itself. They may for the moment be useful
in beating civilized people into submission, but if
there is enough resolution left in the civilized world
to resist this decadence it must ultimately contribute
to the downfall of Germany itself. Unless every
vestige of decency has been destroyed in Germany
it will be impossible to maintain the morale of a
once civilized people by the cynicism of the Nazi
creed. Hitler's hysterical insistence that he is merely
redressing the injustices of Versailles, even while
he conceives plans for world dominion, are the tribute
which his imperial ambitions must pay to what is
left of a sense of justice in this once civilized community.

IV

A primitive community finally has a provisional
advantage over civilized nations in the self-sufficiency
of its economic and cultural life. The national will-
to-live is not distracted by the supernational interests and loyalties which disturb more enlightened
communities; and a national economy of *Autarkie*
is not as seriously dislocated by war as the economy
of the more interdependent nations, because it has
been placed upon a war footing in peace time. The

initial advantage of such a spiritual and economic self-sufficiency is enormous. Combined with the advantages of autocratic power, they have enabled Hitler to throw the resources of seven years of military preparation into one supreme military thrust and have resulted in the collapse of the French nation.

If, however, Britain should be able to parry the German thrust and if America should be able to overcome the weaknesses of civilized virtues and vices sufficiently to participate in this struggle before it is too late, the German advantages will finally disappear. The economics of *Autarkie* have been purchased at the price of the impoverishment of a whole nation. A nation which has been asked to bear the privations of war for years before overt hostilities broke out is bound to succumb to weariness before its foes, if its foes can withstand the initial thrust of the lethal weapons which have been fashioned at the expense of a nation's living standards.

Furthermore the decadent cultural self-sufficiency has little in common with the primitive and natural self-centeredness of a barbaric community. The one is as different from the other as the egocentricity of a psychopathic differs from the egocentricity of a child. The Germans are momentarily so sure of themselves in their triumph because they are not sure of themselves at all. Their inferiority complex has a voracious appetite and requires constant victories to satisfy it. The religion of collective self-worship by which the modern Germans compensate their sense of inferiority and with which they have supplanted the Christian religion, undoubtedly gives them a demonic vitality for the moment. It was sufficient to overwhelm the French nation, but it may be questioned whether it will suffice to overwhelm the British Empire.

The British have been weakened by all the vices and virtues of civilization which we have enumerated. Their long centuries of comparative internal stability and external security vitiated their will-to-live and subjected them to all the complacent illusions to which civilized communities are prone. But they have a much stronger internal cohesion than the French or for that matter than our own country. Their sense of the organic aspects of human existence has never atrophied to the degree manifested in other parts of the democratic world. Inasfar as morale will determine the outcome of the struggle the morale of British civilization has more solid foundations than German morale and will prevail, always provided that Germany does not overwhelm Britain in its initial thrust.

In short the vitalities of a "faked" and synthetic barbarism may have a tremendous might. They present civilized communities with an appalling peril. They may prevail and throw our whole civilization into the darkness of barbarism. But if they do not prevail quickly they cannot prevail at all. They represent the demonic fury of the possessed, who, freed of the cautions and inhibitions which check the normal spirit, are able to concentrate all their energy in a moment of effort. Should that effort succeed they might conceivably reduce the whole of civilization to their level. Whether they succeed or not depends upon the degree of health which the undefeated portions of civilization still maintain.

There is no portion of western civilization which does not suffer from both the vices and the illusions of civilized communities. In fact the sentimental illusions to which highly civilized and stable communities are prone have been accentuated in our western history, by the utopianism of the eighteenth century which mistook the momentary stability of an expanding capitalistic society for the final peace of the Kingdom of God. If such a civilization is saved it will only be because it learned in the final hour of crisis to purge itself of its illusions and to recognize the precarious character of all historic achievements.

10

THE FALSE ANSWERS TO OUR

UNSOLVED PROBLEMS

THE SECOND WORLD WAR must be regarded as both a revelation and a consequence of the total crisis in which Western civilization stands. The Nazis represent the sickness of our culture and civilization in the most virulent form; but it is obvious that they could not have come to power first in Germany and then in Europe if the whole of our Western civilization had not been very sick.

German fascism is both a consequence of, and an effort to remedy, the economic sickness of our society. The world depression was the final force which brought Hitler to power. The Nazis solved the unemployment problem by harnessing the total resources of the nation to the military task. The wealthier nations were not driven to the same desperate expedients; but it is significant that Britain overcame its unemployment problem only after it began to arm to meet the Nazi threat, and that even then it did not absorb the total number of its unemployed. In the same way our own nation, though not at war, is more and more tempted to seek a momentary solution of unemployment by large-scale military expenditures.

If peace should come, all modern nations — whether victors, neutrals, or vanquished—will face the basic problems of a technical civilization in a more acute form than ever. About the only advantage which we will have from the experiences of the past two decades is the knowledge that neither fascism nor communism is a healthy alternative to the sickness of capitalist society. The former was supposed by radicals to be an effort to preserve private property, while the latter was assumed to have solved the problem through the abolition of private property. The Nazis have proved themselves not too interested in the preservation of private property. One of their angels, Fritz Thyssen, has lost all his property, and "bolshevization from the top," the emergence of a kind of military communism, is a real probability in Germany. Russia has proved, on the other hand, that the ownership of property is not the only form of irresponsible power which creates injustice. All ownership might be abolished; but if the right to control property remains in the hands of an essentially irresponsible oligarchy the net result is merely to merge political and economic power in the hands of one oligarchy.

Such justice as we have in capitalistic democracies is partly derived from our ability to check one kind of power by another. The Russian and German alternatives to capitalistic decay are approaching each other not only in terms of the nationalistic imperialistic motives of their foreign policy but in terms of the bastard military communism of their domestic economic policy. In this connection one must observe that Trotsky's defense of the Russian aggression against Finland is a pathetic piece of "ideology." Forced by his simple Marxist creed to believe that the abolition of capitalism also means the abolition of imperialism, he is persuaded to regard Russia as an essentially healthy society which is momentarily in the hands of traitors; but he condones the actions of these same traitors because his faith does not permit him to entertain the idea that an essentially communist society could really do wrong.

It ought to be particularly significant for those who hold a Christian faith and who look at the world in terms of Christian insights that political issues are continually confused by all sorts of simple illusions, all of which contain the basic illusion that it is possible for some group of men or nations, either by virtue of superior intelligence or by virtue of a superior economic organization, to overcome the sinfulness of the human heart and achieve some vantage point of perfection from which they can look down upon the evil world.

German fascism is also a consequence and an effort to remedy the political anarchy of our Western civilization. This anarchy expressed itself particularly in the peace of Versailles, partly through the fact that the vindictive emotions of the World War made it impossible to achieve a decent peace, partly because the most potent symbol of justice which guided the peacemakers at Versailles, "the self-determination of nations," was too negative, too individualistic and particularistic to do justice to the unity of Europe.

The injustice of Versailles to the Germans has been very much overstated. The territorial provisions of Versailles were wrong not because they were unjust but because they were untenable. Only the indemnity clauses and the war guilt clause of the treaty were really unjust. The real difficulty was that the new nations which the treaty rightfully created could not maintain themselves in the end against a resurgent German nationalism. This problem of the small nations of Europe is symbolic of the whole problem of national sovereignty in a highly interdependent world.

The fascist and communist alternatives to this nationalistic particularism are as false as their alternatives to the economic problem. The Germans hoped to unify Europe in terms of making German imperialism the organizing center of that unity. They might actually have succeeded if their imperialism had had a little more sense of justice in it. Even then German imperialism would not have been an ideal solution. But it is absurd to think of the Nazis, with their destructive fury and cruelty and their total disregard of the rights of other nations, as instruments of unity for the anarchy of Europe.

Interestingly enough, the communist effort to abolish nations is as false as Nazi imperialism and, though standing in logical contradiction to it, actually begins to approach it in method. Which proves how life may negate logic. If one begins with the illusion that nationalism is merely the product of capitalism and that a communist society is by definition free of the sentiment of nationality and the temptation to imperialism, vigilance against these perils is relaxed and thus the way is opened for a not too covert Russian nationalistic imperialism to insinuate itself into the revolutionary cause. So powerful is the force of the communist dogma that there are still millions of believers in nations outside Russia who deny the most obvious historical facts so that they may cling to their dogmatic illusions. One is reminded of the fact that the French Revolution once falsely identified nationalism with the dynastic principle, imagined a bourgeois idealism free of this bigotry and thus paved the way for the unholy compound of bourgeois idealism and French nationalistic passion under Napoleon.

There is something rather pathetic about the perennial emergence of these false solutions, all of which have one element in common. They assume that our own particular type of idealism has permanently destroyed certain evils of history, which continue to pop up in new forms and disguises. They falsely identify basic evils of human history with a particular evil, as exhibited in the life of the foe.

Culturally the crisis of Western civilization expresses itself in the substitution of secular religions for the insights of a genuine Christian faith. The cultural decay of Western Christendom is older than the economic and political decay. The symbol for that is the fact that German religious nationalism has cultural antecedents in German romanticism, decades before there was a World War and a world depression. German nationalism is the cheapest and most dangerous sort of secular religion. It is simply the resurgence of tribal polytheism, expressed in virulent form because it is a complete anachronism. It cannot gain the allegiance of modern men without creating a perverse primitivism, and it cannot be introduced into the unities of an interdependent civilization without creating anarchy.

The communist alternative seemed to all of us to be of a higher order. It was a kind of secularized prophetic religion. It enshrined a principle of universalism rather than one of particularism. It dreamed of a just and a universal society. Here again life has sadly dissipated radiant hopes. This degeneration proves how dangerous all secular religions are. A messianic class may become as evil as a messianic nation. Nothing is more true than that the working class stands, or stood, under a very special historic destiny. But if there is not some transcendent reference from which a particular historical mission is judged, the executors of divine judgment in history vainly imagine themselves to be God, even if they do not believe in God—or perhaps particularly if they do not believe in God. The struggle between the prophets and the pride of Israel, in which the prophets sought vainly to prove to Israel that a nation might have a special mission and yet not be immune to the divine judgment, contains ultimate insights which are completely lost in modern life.

Thus a potentially creative movement degenerates into something not very different from an obvious reversion to the primitive.

Such is the state of our confusion and decay in Western civilization. Obviously there is no simple way back to health from a disease with so many complications. The defeat of Nazi Germany is a *sine qua non* of health, though obviously it is only a negative condition of health. Suggestions that the triumph of Naziism would have been better than a war or that it would be better to come to terms with the Nazis now rather than continue the war, suggestions which continue to emanate from sources which hold to the dogmatic position that war is worse than even the worst tyranny, have little relation to the realities. A virulent tyranny is worse than war because it comprehends both the present destruction of culture as an immediate consequence and war as an ultimate consequence. Tyrannies are not destroyed without being resisted; and they are resisted in the end when their exactions have become unbearable or when always unbearable exactions have driven their victims to the fury of vengeance.

The defeat of Germany, difficult as that now seems, is however only the negative condition of a new Europe. The task will then still remain to create a new Europe, to develop a new system of national interdependence, to abridge national sovereignty sufficiently to accomplish this purpose, to eliminate national barriers to trade, and to achieve a higher degree of justice within each nation. These tasks are so great individually and collectively that they may well strike terror into the frail of heart. If they cannot be achieved, Western civilization must sink further into decay.

11

MODERN UTOPIANS

I T IS UNFORTUNATE THAT social controversy in critical periods of history should be unnecessarily aggravated and the mind of nations be needlessly confused by the hypocrisy of the tories and the utopianism of the radicals. The former affect to believe that the imperilled society which they are defending is the only possible basis of social peace and progress while the latter, with greater sincerity but with no more truth, insist that the new social forms which they advocate will cure society of all its ills. History proves both similar fears and similar hopes to be groundless.

In our contemporary situation the capitalists insist that only their social organization can provide adequate incentives for social co-operation and furnish the necessary mechanism of social cohesion. Their theory that the hope of profit is the only adequate motive of socially useful toil is belied by the fact that the vast majority of men in a capitalistic society perform their several functions without the inspiration of such a hope. Their contention that capitalistic social organization automatically makes for mutual accord and social peace is disproved by every event of contemporary history in which the inherent anarchy of the system and its inability to preserve peace and security are revealed by cumulative evidence. Yet even the most convincing proof does not prevent consistent tories from regretting whatever concessions to the ideal of social control they may have made or have been forced to make, and from contending that a relaxation of this control would heal their sick society. This argument is rationally so absurd that one is forced to conclude, as indeed all history proves, that imperilled oligarchies are neither able nor willing to think clearly and honestly; and that their dishonesties are frequently so patent and blatant that they must be attributed to conscious perversity rather than unconscious self-deception.

The confusion in the thought of the radicals arises from a different source. Their romantic utopianism is the consequence of the tension under which rebels against an established society and traditional values must live. The leaders of radicalism spend their lives in analyzing the defects of the system which they seek to overthrow; and the rank and file of their followers are the victims of these defects in their own experience. Both therefore naturally incline to attribute every evil to which the human flesh is heir solely to the particular social organization which they seek to transmute or destroy. Furthermore the hope of a millennium is the natural dream of all souls sensitive enough to feel the injustices of the hour keenly. Injustice is not challenged if justice is not felt to be a reality. Since it is not a present reality it must be given a locus in either the past or the future of history. Sober thought ought to convince even the purest idealist that history relativizes all ideals; but robust social action, particularly rebellious action, is not always the fruit of sober thought. Men seem to require the intoxication of the vision of the absolute if they are to contend robustly against malignant power.

The utopianism of the eighteenth century persuaded its dreamers to expect the millennium as the fruit of universal suffrage and universal education. Their dreams ended in disillusionment and gave us the sorry realities of our day. Now we are in the process of learning that the equalization of political power does not yield justice if the more potent economic power is left disproportionately in the hands of a few and allowed to bend political power to its will: nor that increasing the literacy of citizens will

143

give them a perfect defense against their oppressors as long as the latter control the organs which mould public opinion.

Disillusionment in democracy may persuade our generation that all dreams of perfect justice are vain; but it must also encourage us to analyze the problem of justice anew. If this is done, no conclusion is more obvious than the conviction that injustice is the inevitable fruit of irresponsible and disproportionate power, that economic power is the most significant and basic form of power in modern society and that relative justice therefore depends upon the socialization of this type of power.

Thus modern society progresses naturally from the democratic to the socialistic hope. The socialistic hope is valid not as the augury of a perfect society but as the promise of the only possible social organization compatible with the necessities of a technical age. The high degree of mechanical interdependence of a technical civilization becomes insufferable if the mechanisms of our social life are under the control of private individuals who, by virtue of the power of ownership, are able to prefer personal advantage to communal welfare in their manipulation of the social process.

This conclusion would be much more obvious if socialists and communists did not obscure it by making impossible utopian claims for the policy of social ownership and promise a society free of every form of social conflict and tyranny. The symbol of communist utopianism is its theory of the withering away of the State. The State, according to communist theory, is not a necessary organ of social cohesion but only a tool of class oppression. It is used by the bourgeoisie for the oppression of the workers and it will be used by the workers for the suppression of the capitalists; but once the process of liquidating the class foes of the workers is accomplished, the need of coercion in social life will disappear and gradually a state of ideal anarchy will emerge in which each will give according to his ability and take according to his need.

The theory of the withering away of the State is based upon the assumption that both the collective egoism of nations and the egoism of individuals are solely the fruit of the class organization of society. The theory therefore assumes that in a classless society no coercion will ultimately be required to harmonize the conflicting interests of men and no danger will exist that the will-to-live and the will-to-power of national units in an international society will come in conflict with each other. There is nothing in the evidence of history to justify the belief that the historic class organization of society is alone responsible for the tendency of men and societies to take advantage of each other. It would be truer to say that the class organization is a consequence of this tendency in the human heart. It may therefore be checked and minimized but not abolished in a society in which power is equalized and held under social control.

It would be unfair to Marxism to suggest that it regards its dictatorship of the proletariat as the Utopia of its dreams. Marx declares: "In a higher phase of communist society, when the enslaving subordination of individuals in the division of labor has disappeared, and with it also the antagonism between mental and physical labor—when along with the all-round development of individuals, the productive forces too have grown and the springs of wealth are flowing more freely, it is only at that stage that it will be possible to pass beyond the narrow horizon of 'bourgeois' rights and for a society to inscribe on its banners: from each according to his ability and to each according to his needs."

The transition period is envisaged as a time of preparation for the Utopia. The proof of its transitional character lies in the fact that it still deals with "rights" though it enforces equal rights. Lenin declares: "Bourgeois rights with respect to distribution of articles of consumption inevitably presuppose of course the existence of the bourgeois State, for rights are nothing without an apparatus capable of enforcing the observance of rights.—Consequently for a certain time not only bourgeois rights but even the bourgeois

State remains under communism without the bourgeoisie." The only difference from the old bourgeois State will be that it will enforce equality: "Immediately after the attainment of equality for all members of society in respect of the ownership of the means of production, that is, of equality of wages and equality of labor, there will inevitably arise for humanity the question of going from formal to real equality.—The whole of society will have become one office and one factory with equal work and equal pay. But this factory discipline is by no means our ideal or our final aim. It is but a foothold—to advance farther. From the moment that all members of society or even only the overwhelming majority have learned to govern the State themselves—from this moment the need for any government begins to disappear."

It is very clear from this logic that the ultimate anarchism of communism justifies itself by attributing all tendencies of men to take advantage of each other to their corruption by the "bourgeois spirit." Thus every temptation to injustice in modern Russia is attributed to the vestigial remnants of the capitalistic spirit and justifies the maximization of the power of the very State which is ultimately to wither away.

That the bourgeois spirit should survive in a State in which there are no bourgeoisie is admitted by Lenin to be one of those "dialectical puzzles" the understanding of which is hidden from the wise and revealed to the babes who have imbibed the pure milk of dialectic philosophy. The utopianism of communism is thus not a mere harmless overbelief. It rests upon an insupportable analysis of the human and social situation, and must inevitably result in a political strategy which needlessly intensifies the social struggle. The inevitable tendency of human beings to be more interested in their own needs than in those of others and to prefer their advantage to that of others, the natural egoism of the human heart, in short, is falsely attributed solely to the capitalistic system. As a consequence every revelation of it gives a proletarian dictatorship a new reason for sharpening its force and seeking to destroy its class enemies. It furthermore prompts complete blindness to the problem of the temptation under which the man of power stands in any civilization whether he be capitalistic oligarch or communistic commissar. The strong equalitarian tradition of Russian communism prevents its leaders from using their political position to profit materially. But greed is not the only root of social injustice. The will-to-power is a form of egoism which has at times tempted ascetic abbots, totally free of the sin of greed, to maintain a vexatious and tyrannical rule over their monks and there is no reason to believe that ascetic commissars would be totally immune to such temptations.

148

The belief that a dictatorship ultimately destroys itself by destroying the "bourgeois" egoism which makes it necessary can have no other consequence than to relax the vigilance of society upon its oligarchy or even to prompt the illusion that its oligarchy is saved by some mystical union with the "rank and file" from succumbing to temptations which have assailed men of power through all the ages. If history teaches any lesson rather conclusively it is that an oligarchy, whether priestly, military, capitalistic or communistic, is not to be trusted, if no form of social control is maintained over it. Democracy as a method of arbitrating social conflict may fail in moments of crisis but democracy as a form of social control upon the leaders of society is a perennial necessity of justice. There have been oligarchies before the communistic one, which, in their creative period, were closely identified with their people and only slightly tempted to prefer their pride to the commonweal; and there will be oligarchies after the communistic one among whom this temptation will become insuperable, after the first fine careless rapture of the creative era is dissipated.

The error of communism in attributing all egoism to capitalistic society can never be fully disproved to the complete devotee as long as he can appeal to the future for possible validation. But in one respect events in Russia have already discredited Marx and

Lenin's description of the transitional period from capitalism to communism. There was to be absolute equality of wage in this period. This formal equality was regarded as falling short of real equality because the needs of men differed. "Different people are not alike," said Lenin, "one is strong, another weak, one is married, the other not, one has more children and the other less." The real equality which would take cognizance of unequal needs would be achieved only in the anarchistic millennium and not in the period in which "bourgeois" rights still prevailed.

The developments in Russia do not fulfill this hope of formal equality in the transitional period. Wage differentials and bonuses are rising to constantly higher heights. While some of them are not available for members of the party, yet the one hundred and fifty ruble per month maximum wage for party members has long since doubled and trebled. It is still denied that this is a necessary concession of communist policy to ineradicable tendencies in human nature. The theory is that the policy is a concession to the capitalistic spirit and will cease to be necessary when that spirit has been eradicated. The theory fails to recognize that the hope of a higher wage may be an incentive to diligence even in a society in which the "capitalistic spirit" has been completely destroyed. It would remain efficacious as long as the family is not completely absorbed in the total society: and the

hope of securing some special advantage for their
family prompted men to a greater diligence than
their concern for the community as such. A wise society will seek to prevent this family loyalty from
becoming a new source of injustice; but the hope of
eliminating it completely springs from an abstract
rationalism which is unable to deal realistically with
the organic relationships of life.

Failure to deal with the organic aspects of life is
probably the root of the utopian internationalism of
communism as well as of its utopian anarchism. Communist theory envisages an ultimate world community of socialist societies in which no single nation
will ever be tempted to profit at the expense of another nation. Imperialism, a form of collective egoism
and will-to-power, is, like individual egoism, attributed solely to capitalism. With the destruction of
capitalism international rivalries will ultimately cease
and a world culture will develop.

John Strachey expresses the utopian internationalism of communism in words which cannot be
misunderstood. "It must not be supposed that communists consider the existence of separate national
cultures, separate languages, and the like, will be a
permanent feature of fully developed world communism. Such phenomena belong to the present, not
to the ultimate stage of human development. It is
clear that man will in the end tire of the inconvenient

idiosyncrasies of locality and will wish to pool the cultural heritage of the human race into a world synthesis." The concept of "inconvenient idiosyncrasies of locality" is typical of rationalistic utopianism. By this and other similar concepts communism reveals its kinship with the utopians of the eighteenth century. The communist differs from the liberal only in finding the source of an evil irrationality not in the ignorance of the individual mind, but in the defect of a social organization.

The fact that all life in its givenness and in its variety is irrational, and that mind and reason are too much the frail flowers which grow upon the stem of this organic life to be able to transcend it completely, invalidates all this rational utopianism. The flowers do indeed turn their faces to the universal sun, but they do not lose the irrational variety of color which nature has given them. French, German, English and other languages are no doubt "inconvenient idiosyncrasies of locality," but just how would one go about creating a rational universal language, or persuade men to accept it, if one could create it? It is true of course that there are universal human experiences which make the whole world kin. But they hardly provide for a "synthesis of world cultures." The greatest art which expresses and illumines these experiences always has its roots solidly in some particular and specific culture and reaches the universal only in some final and transcendent expression of spirituality.

The idea of a completely harmonious world civilization is as utopian as the expectation of a universal synthesis of cultures. Capitalism undoubtedly aggravates international animosities by tempting each nation to save itself from the chaos of its faulty distribution of wealth by seeking to sell other nations more than it is willing or able to buy from them. This particular cause of international friction will disappear with the passing of capitalism. Nations capable of consuming roughly as much goods as they produce can achieve a greater mutuality of exchange with other nations than is possible for the capitalistic nations at the present moment. But wars between nations and other social units are older than capitalism; and the will-to-power of a strong nation can express itself in other terms than the desire to exploit the economic resources of weaker nations. Napoleonic imperialism was compounded of national pride and fanatic devotion to the cause of the bourgeois revolution. Occasions for such "spiritual" imperialism might conceivably disappear in a world in which socialism or communism had been universally accepted. But such a world is very remote. Meanwhile it is as unrealistic to attribute imperial ambition in nations only to their greed as to identify the will-to-power of individuals solely with their desire to gain material advantages.

Even if a uniform social system throughout the world destroyed the possibility of uniting devotion to political principles with national sentiment, there is no reason to believe that any single unit of a world socialist society would be so wise and so good as never to be tempted to seek advantages at the expense of the total community, or that a world government would always have the prestige and the power to prevent the antisocial conduct of some recalcitrant member of the international society. The idea that a world government is merely a rational extension of the principle of federation, as applied to the development of the United States for instance, is one of those rationalistic illusions which takes no account of the limited resources of reason in transcending the perspective, prejudices, and interests of limited communities.

The answer of utopians to such pessimistic apprehensions is always the same, whether it proceeds from liberal or radical romanticists. They declare that pessimistic reservations upon their utopian dreams are predicated upon the assumption that human nature does not change, while it is their belief that human nature is surprisingly malleable and is to a large degree the product of its environment. The question is whether they have not confused human nature with human behavior. Human behavior is constantly changing under the influence of various

154

stimuli. The difference in the behavior of a Chinese Buddhist monk, a British aristocrat, a Prussian general, an American go-getter, an expatriated artist, and a Russian worker is very considerable. But a certain common human nature underlies all this varied behavior. Its common characteristics have been obscured by the rationalistic illusions which began in the eighteenth century, and which lost sight of common human traits in their emphasis upon the variable factors of education and environment.

The basic and unchangeable factor in human character is that human reason is on the one hand conditioned and limited by the circumstances of time, place, climate, and every other natural limitation, and is on the other hand capable of transcending self and environment in a practically infinite series of rational and moral judgments. Man is a child of nature and finitude. The Marxian theory of economic determinism is true, but is only part of the truth. Man's ideas are conditioned not only by the means of production upon which he depends and the economic interests which he seeks to defend; they are also conditioned by racial history, geographic influences, family traditions, and every conceivable partial perspective of a mind imbedded in a finite organism. Yet this creature of finitude touches the fringes of the infinite, and every awakened human mind searches for the universally valid value and the unconditioned truth.

The assumption of rationalists in the past centuries has been that either education or the equalization of economic interests would finally fashion the mind into a perfect instrument of universal and absolute knowledge, and would ultimately destroy social friction by eliminating the partial perspectives which prompt men to assess social issues in conflicting terms. But this assumption fails to recognize that the most intelligent and disinterested person can never escape his fate as a child of nature and finitude. The same intelligence which provides universal rather than partial perspectives must inevitably also operate to give partial perspectives the authority of the absolute. Thus even the most refined spiritual achievements of humanity can never result in an unqualified synthesis of human hopes and aspirations. At some point they will always accentuate social conflict by making men more stubborn in the defense of their interests, under the illusion that their interests represent universal values. That is one reason why modern warfare is more terrible than the wars of primitive men.

To the honest self-deceptions of men, who are so curiously suspended between finitude and the universal, must be added an element of dishonesty which arises from the force of the human ego's will-to-live and will-to-power. This egoism is stronger in men than in beasts precisely because man is the only finite creature who knows that he is finite and he is therefore tempted to protest against his fate. One form which this protest takes is his imperialistic ambition, his effort to overcome his insignificance by subordinating other life to his individual or collective will. He naturally seeks both the consent of his own conscience and the acquiescence of his victims by hiding his own interests behind universal values. It is interesting, incidentally, that Marxian theory of class interests explicitly denies any conscious dishonesty in the moral and cultural pretensions of class imperialism while Marxian political strategy arouses a perfect fury of contempt for the moral dishonesties of its foes. These dishonesties belong to the permanent spiritual problem of man.

The spiritual structure of human character is, in short, of such a nature that it is preposterous to hope that an individual will can ever be inserted with frictionless harmony into a general community will or that a national will can, under any conceivable circumstances, be brought completely under the dominion of a world society. These hopes are preposterous for the simple reason that the very capacities in human life which make for progress and for social integration upon higher and higher levels also make it certain that an individual or a collective ego will and must, on occasion, defy the community. Cæsars and saints are made possible by the same structure of human character. Human progress is possible only because some human spirits will on occasion transcend the presuppositions of their society and envisage more perfect goals for life than their society has been able to comprehend. This very capacity will always make it possible for imperial individuals and groups to arise and seek to subordinate life to their will and purpose. Whether their imperialism is the consequence of an honest deception or whether it is dishonestly compounded of the egoistic will-to-power and the human spirit's search for universal values, the inevitable expression of these imperial wills is guaranteed in the very structure of human character. Upon it all utopian dreams of perfect harmony will be shattered.

Modern technical society is desperately in need of the socialization of economic power in order that it may minimize the injustices which result inevitably from endowing the anarchic ego with unlimited power over other life. That the proponents of this necessary social change should confuse the issues by falsely claiming to be the instruments of a perfect society and of a universal culture is itself one of those manifestations of the fateful human tendency to confuse the immediate and the ultimate. Radical theories have no understanding for this perennial problem of the human spirit; but radical social strategy offers abundant proof of its universality.

12

HITLER AND BUCHMAN

On RETURNING FROM Europe, Frank Buchman, Oxford group revivalist, is quoted by a reputable New York paper as having said: "I thank heaven for a man like Adolf Hitler, who built a front-line defense against the anti-Christ of communism. . . . My barber in London told me Hitler saved all Europe from communism. That's how he felt. Of course I don't condone everything the Nazis do. Antisemitism? Bad, naturally. I suppose Hitler sees a Karl Marx in every Jew. But think what it would mean to the world if Hitler surrendered to the control of God. Or Mussolini. Or any dictator. Through such a man God could control a nation overnight and solve every last bewildering problem."

In this interview the social philosophy of the Oxford group, long implicit in its strategy, is made explicit, and revealed in all its childishness and viciousness. This philosophy has been implicit in Buchmanite strategy from the beginning. It explains the particular attention which is paid by Mr. Buchman and his followers to big men, leaders, in industry and politics. The idea is that if the man of power can be converted, God will be able to control a larger area of human life through his power than if a little man were converted. This is the logic which has filled the Buchmanites with touching solicitude for the souls of such men as Henry Ford or Harvey Firestone and prompted them to whisper confidentially from time to time that these men were on the very threshold of the kingdom of God. It is this strategy which prompts or justifies the first-class travel of all the Oxford teams. They hope to make contact with big men in the luxurious first-class quarters of ocean liners.

A NAZI PHILOSOPHY

In other words, a Nazi social philosophy has been a covert presupposition of the whole Oxford group enterprise from the very beginning. We may be grateful to the leader for revealing so clearly what has been slightly hidden. Now we can see how unbelievably naïve this movement is in its efforts to save the world. If it would content itself with preaching repentance to drunkards and adulterers one might be willing to respect it as a religious revival method which knows how to confront the sinner with God. But when it runs to Geneva, the seat of the League of Nations, or to Prince Starhemberg or Hitler, or to any seat of power, always with the idea that it is on the verge of saving the world by bringing the people who control the world under God-control, it is difficult to restrain the contempt which one feels for this dangerous childishness.

This idea of world salvation implies a social philosophy which is completely innocent of any understanding of the social dynamics of a civilization. Does Mr. Buchman really believe that the dictators of the modern world create their dictatorships out of whole cloth? He does not know, evidently, that they are the creatures more than the creators of vast social movements in modern history. The particular social forces which create dictatorships are on the whole the decadent forces of a very sick society. The sickness of that society is the sickness of sin; and if a word of God is to be spoken in such an hour as this let it be the woe of Christ upon his Jerusalem or the prophecy of judgment which an Amos or Jeremiah pronounced upon their civilization.

THE PRODUCT OF THE QUIET HOUR

There is unfortunately not the slightest indication that the prophetic spirit of the Bible has ever entered into this pollyanna religion by way of the quiet hour. Several times Mr. Buchman has confessed that the word of God which he heard in his quiet hour was the slogan: "An international network over spiritual live-wires," whatever that may mean. In other words, the world is to be saved by a vulgar advertising slogan rather than by a genuine priestly and prophetic mediation of the judgment and the mercy of God upon a sinful world.

The Oxford group's interpretation of modern history is not only unbelievably naïve in dealing with the social dynamics of a tragic era. It is definitely unbiblical in its approach to men of power. If we granted for the moment that dictators were really the creators rather than the creatures of the social forces of the modern day and if we regarded their power as a simple personal force, exerted without complexity upon their social order, what could we preach to these men in terms of the gospel? The most relevant word would be: "Not many wise men after the flesh, not many mighty, not many noble are called." If that word were taken seriously by the Oxford group it might incidentally tend to discourage house parties in all the fashionable summer resorts where the mighty and the noble, though hardly the wise, congregate.

THE MAN OF POWER

In the simple and decadent individualism of the Oxford group movement there is no understanding of the fact that the man of power is always to a certain degree an anti-Christ. "All power," said Lord Acton with cynical realism, "corrupts; and absolute power corrupts absolutely." If the man of power were to take a message of absolute honesty and absolute love seriously he would lose his power, or would divest himself of it. This is not to imply that the world can get along without power and that it is not preferable that men of conscience should wield it rather than scoundrels. But if men of power had not only conscience but also something of the gospel's insight into the intricacies of social sin in the world, they would know that they could never extricate themselves completely from the sinfulness of power, even while they were wielding it ostensibly for the common good.

Mr. Buchman has greater aptness for advertising slogans than for historical perspectives. Otherwise he might have had occasion to meditate upon the life of Oliver Cromwell. Cromwell was a Christian in the real sense. There was a vital Christian faith in him which is hardly available for a modern statesman even after the ministrations of the Oxford group. Cromwell really wanted to do the will of God—and thought he was doing it. Yet nothing in Cromwell's personal religion could save his dictatorship from being abortive and self-devouring. Let Mr. Buchman read about Cromwell's campaign in Ireland and the religious pretensions he made for his ambitions there and learn something of the moral complexities which men of power face and the temptations to which they succumb. It might be added that Cromwell's genuine religion not only failed to make his dictatorship palatable; it also failed to save him from the personal temptation to arrogance and cruelty.

The life and religion of Bismarck suggest similar lessons. Bismarck, who established a slightly more palatable dictatorship in Germany than Hitler's, was a convert of the pietist movement. This movement was informed by an evangelical fervor which some of us may be pardoned for preferring to the sentimentalities of the Oxford groups. It deeply affected Bismarck. He was in certain areas of his life a very genuine Christian. But his surrender to God hardly accomplished the results in politics which Mr. Buchman envisages as a possibility in the case of Hitler's conversion. It did not help God to "control his nation overnight and solve every last bewildering problem."

The increasingly obvious fascist philosophy which informs the group movement is in other words not only socially vicious but religiously vapid. The slightest acquaintance with the history of Christian thought on the problem of the relation of the absolute demands of the gospel to the relativities of politics and economics would prove its childishness. A careful study of the gospel itself, particularly its abhorrence of the self-righteousness of the righteous, would reveal the danger of any doctrine which promises powerful men the possibility of fully doing the will of God. They had better be admonished that after they have done what they think right they will still remain unprofitable servants.

The Oxford group movement, imagining itself the mediator of Christ's salvation in a catastrophic age, is really an additional evidence of the decay in which we stand. Its religion manages to combine bourgeois complacency with Christian contrition in a manner which makes the former dominant. Its morality is a religious expression of a decadent individualism. Far from offering us a way out of our difficulties it adds to the general confusion. This is not the gospel's message of judgment and hope to the world. It is bourgeois optimism, individualism and moralism expressing itself in the guise of religion. No wonder the rather jittery plutocrats of our day open their spacious summer homes to its message!

13

AN END TO ILLUSIONS

HE MORNING NEWSPAPER
brings reports of disaster everywhere. The morning
mail acquaints me with the confusion created by these
reports. My mail this morning, for example, contains
four significant communications. The first is a letter
from the Socialist Party informing me that my views
on foreign affairs violate the party platform and asking me to give account of my nonconformity. The
party position is that this war is a clash of rival imperialisms in which nothing significant is at stake. The
second letter asks me to support an organization
which will bring peace to the world by establishing
"world education" and erecting a "world radio." It
fails to explain how its world education is to seep into
the totalitarian states and wean them from their
mania. The third letter is from a trade union under

167

Communist influence asking me to speak at a union "peace" meeting. The fourth is from a parson who wants me to join in an effort to set "moral force against Hitler's battalions," but it fails to explain just how this moral force is to be effective against tanks, flame-throwers, and bombing planes.

This mail increases the melancholy prompted by the morning's news. I answer the Socialist communication by a quick resignation from the party. I inform the trade union that my views would not be acceptable at its peace meeting. The proposal for a world radio is quickly consigned to a file which already contains eighty-two different recipes for world salvation. I start to answer the parson who wants to set "moral force" against Hitler, but overcome with a sense of futility and doubting my ability to penetrate the utopian fog in which the letter was conceived, I throw my reply into the wastebasket. Thus I save some time to meditate upon the perspective which informs this whole morning's mail and upon the vapid character of the culture which Hitler intends to destroy. This culture does not understand historical reality clearly enough to deserve to survive. It has a right to survival only because the alternative is too horrible to contemplate. All four letters are but expressions of the utopianism which has informed our Western world since the eighteenth century.

The Socialists have a dogma that this war is a clash

of rival imperialisms. Of course they are right. So is
a clash between myself and a gangster a conflict of
rival egotisms. There is a perspective from which
there is not much difference between my egotism
and that of a gangster. But from another perspective
there is an important difference. "There is not much
difference between people," said a farmer to William
James, "but what difference there is is very important." That is a truth which the Socialists in America
have not yet learned. The Socialists are right, of
course, in insisting that the civilization which we are
called upon to defend is full of capitalistic and imperialistic injustice. But it is still a civilization. Utopianism creates confusion in politics by measuring all
significant historical distinctions against purely ideal
perspectives and blinding the eye to differences which
may be matters of life and death in a specific instance.

The Socialists rightly call attention to the treason
of the capitalistic oligarchy which has brought the
cause of democracy to so desperate a state. But we are
defending something which transcends the interests of
Mr. Chamberlain and the venality of M. Bonnet.
Furthermore, the Socialists have forgotten how much
they contributed to the capitulation of democracy to
tyranny. It was a Socialist Prime Minister, Paul-
Henri Spaak who contrived the unrealistic neutrality
policy of Belgium which was responsible for the German break-through at Sedan. The policy was unreal-

istic because it was based upon the quite untrue assumption that Belgium was imperilled equally by rival imperialistic powers. The peril was not equal at all, and history has avenged this lie in a terrible way. The Socialists of the Scandinavian countries were deeply involved in the parasitic pacifism of these small nations which scorned "power politics" and forgot that their security rested upon the British navy and the contingencies of a precarious balance of power. The Socialists of Britain willed to resist Hitler but did not will the means of resistance. As for Munich, I heard American Socialists give thanks that a madman with a gun was met by a man with an umbrella. If there had been two guns, rather than an umbrella and a gun, they said, the world would have been plunged into conflict. European Socialists have learned to repent of these errors under the pressure of tragic events, leaving only American Socialists to indulge the luxury of their utopianism.

The proposal for "world radio" and "world education" is merely a particularly fatuous form of the utopian rationalism and universalism which have informed the thought of liberal intellectuals in the whole Western world. These liberals have always imagined that it was a comparatively simple matter for the human mind to transcend the welter of interest and passion which is the very stuff of existence. They have not understood that man's very capacity for freedom creates the imperialist will to dominate, as well as the desire to subordinate life to universal standards. The five hundred American scientists who recently presented a memorial to the President favoring neutrality in the name of scientific impartiality seem not to have the slightest idea that scientific freedom is dependent upon the vicissitudes of political history. Their allusions reveal that modern culture completely misunderstands history precisely because it has learned a great deal about nature and falsely imagines that the harmonies and securities of nature are a safe asylum for man.

There seems to be absolutely no end to the illusions of which intellectuals are capable and no height of unrealistic dreaming to which they cannot rise. Aldous Huxley dreams in Hollywood of a method of making man harmless by subtracting or abstracting the self from selfhood, and stumbles into a pseudo-Buddhistic mysticism as the way of salvation without understanding that this kind of mysticism annuls all history in the process of destroying the self.

When the intellectuals are not given to a vapid form of universalism they elaborate an impossible individualism. Bertrand Russell, who has now repented of his pacifism, wrote in an article recently reprinted in *The Nation* that any political view which made individuals the bearers of ideological forces was outmoded.* The fact is that Nazi collectivism with its primitive emphasis upon "blood and soil" is but a cruel and psychopathic emphasis upon organic and collective aspects of life which liberal individualism has outraged. As late as last February the *New Republic* promised to stand resolutely against any moral urge that might carry us into war because it knew so certainly that the "evils of a system" could not be cured by "killing the unfortunate individuals who for a moment embody the system." It failed to tell us that the individuals who for the moment embody a system might possibly fasten a system of slavery upon us which would not be for a moment. When Germany invaded Holland and Belgium and the situation of the western democracies became precarious, the *New Republic* forgot these individualistic scruples and solemnly warned that we could not afford to allow the British navy to be destroyed, though it did not tell us how we were to prevent it without imperilling the lives of unfortunate individual sailors and soldiers "who for the moment embody a system." The real fact is that we have no right to deal with the rough stuff of politics at all if we do not understand that politics always deals with collective action and that collective action invariably involves both

* "What I Believe," in *The Nation*, March 3, 1940.

guilty and guiltless among the individuals who for the moment embody a system.

The letter from the communistic trade union in my mail can stand as a symbol of the aberrations of those who frantically cling to Russia as their hope of salvation. The fear that a triumphant Germany will invade the Ukraine may bring Russia back on the side of the angels shortly, and then the rest of us will be told how wrong we were in judging Russia prematurely. Fortunately, we have no intellectuals of the standing of George Bernard Shaw and J. B. S. Haldane who, under the influence of the Russian obsession, talk such nonsense as these two men have permitted themselves.

The letter from the parson who wanted to set "moral force" against Hitler's battalions is a nice example of the sentimentalized form of Christianity which has engulfed our churches, particularly in America, and which has prompted them to dream of "spiritualizing life" by abstracting spirit from matter, history, and life. It is significant that this kind of "spiritual" religion identifies religious perfectionism with the morally dubious and politically dangerous dogmas of isolation. If we could only keep free of this European struggle we might still indulge our illusions about the character of human existence, which Christianity at its best illumines.

A survey of our culture gives us the uneasy feeling that Hitler was not quite wrong in his boast that he would destroy the world of the eighteenth century. In its more articulate forms our culture suffers from illusions which weaken its will and its right to survive. One can only be grateful for the common sense of common folk which has not been corrupted by these illusions and which in the hour of peril expresses itself in sound political instincts. But for this common sense we might capitulate to a system of government which declares war to be normal, because we do not believe in war. We might submit to a culture which glorifies force as the final arbiter, because we thought it a simple task to extricate reason from force. We might allow a primitive collectivism to enslave us, because we had false ideas of the relation of the individual to the collective forces of life. We might submit to tyranny and the negation of justice, because we had an uneasy conscience about the injustices which corrupt our system of justice.

Hitler threatens the whole world not merely because the democracies were plutocratic and betrayed by their capitalist oligarchies. His victories thus far are partly due to the fact that the culture of the democracies was vapid. Its political instincts had become vitiated by an idealism which sought to extricate morals from politics to the degree of forgetting that all life remains a contest of power. If Hitler is defeated in the end it will be because the crisis has awakened in us the will to preserve a civilization in which jus-

tice and freedom are realities, and given us the knowledge that ambiguous methods are required for the
ambiguities of history. Let those who are revolted by
such ambiguities have the decency and consistency to
retire to the monastery, where medieval perfectionists
found their asylum.

14

OPTIMISM, PESSIMISM AND

RELIGIOUS FAITH—I

Human vitality has two primary sources, animal impulse and confidence in the meaningfulness of human existence. The more human consciousness arises to full self-consciousness and to a complete recognition of the total forces of the universe in which it finds itself, the more it requires not only animal vitality but confidence in the meaningfulness of its world to maintain a healthy will-to-live. This confidence in the meaningfulness of life is not something which results from a sophisticated analysis of the forces and factors which surround the human enterprise. It is something which is assumed in every healthy life. It is primary religion. Men may be quite unable to define the meaning of life, and yet live by a simple trust that it has meaning. This primary religion is the basic optimism of all vital and wholesome human life.

In primitive life the meaning of existence is revealed in the relation of the individual to his group. Life achieves meaning through its organic relation to a social enterprise. This loyalty usually results in some form of totemistic religion which gives a mythical and symbolic expression of the feeling that the value and meaning of the social group really represents absolute meaning. Such totemistic religion remains, in spite of all further elaborations, a permanent source of optimism of some people in all ages and all cultures, who refuse to ask ultimate questions about the relation of the value of their social group to some ultimate source of meaning. Some men achieve a very considerable happiness in their devotion to their family or their community or nation without asking any further questions about life's meaning. When national loyalty is reconstructed into an all-absorbing religion, as in modern Germany, we may witness the recrudescence of primitive religion in the modern period on a large scale.

In spite of the comparative satisfaction of many people, both primitive and modern, in a little cosmos, it is inevitable that men should seek to relate their group to a larger source of meaning just as surely as they must relate themselves to the life of the group. Thus animism is as primordial as totemism in the history of religion. In other words, men tried to bring the world of nature into their universe of meaning from the very beginning, and sought to relate their little cosmos to a larger cosmos. The gradual identification of nature gods with the gods of tribes and cities in the religions of early civilization shows how quickly the social cosmos was related to the larger universe, revealed in the world of nature, and a common center and source of meaning was attributed to both of them.

But the simple faith and optimism of primitive man did not exist long without being challenged. The world is not only a cosmos but a chaos. Every universe of meaning is constantly threatened by meaninglessness. Its harmonies are disturbed by discords. Its self-sufficiency is challenged by larger and more inclusive worlds. The more men think the more they are tempted to pessimism because their thought surveys the worlds which lie beyond their little cosmos, and analyzes the chaos, death, destruction and misery which seem to deny their faith in the harmony and meaningfulness of their existence in it. All profound religion is an effort to answer the challenge of pessimism. It seeks a center of meaning in life which is able to include the totality of existence, and which is able to interpret the chaos as something which only provisionally threatens its cosmos and can ultimately be brought under its dominion.

In the Jewish-Christian tradition this problem of pessimism and optimism is solved by faith in a transcendent God who is at once the creator of the world (source of its meaning) and judge of the world (*i. e.* goal of its perfection). It was this faith in a transcendent God which made it possible for Hebraic religion to escape both the parochial identification of God and the nation and the pantheistic identification of God and the imperfections of historical existence. It provided, in other words, for both the universalism and the perfectionism which are implied in every vital ethics. It is interesting to note that the process of divorcing God from the nation was a matter of both spiritual insight and actual experience. If the early prophets had not said, as Amos, "Are ye not as the children of the Ethiopians unto me, saith the Lord," faith in the God of Israel might have perished with the captivity of Judah. But it was the exile which brought this process to a triumphant conclusion. A second Isaiah could build on the spiritual insights of an Amos, and could declare a God who gave meaning to existence quite independent of the vicissitudes of a nation, which had been the chief source of all meaning to the pious Jew.

In the same manner faith in a transcendent God made it possible to affirm confidence in a meaningful existence even though the world was full of sorrow and evil. Some of the sorrow and misery was attributed to human sin. It was because man sinned that thorns and thistles grew in his field and he was forced to earn his bread by the sweat of his brow. The myth of the fall may solve the problem of evil too easily by attributing all inadequacies of nature to the imperfections of man, but it contains one element of truth found in all profound religion, and that is that it reduces man's pride and presumption in judging the justice of the universe by making him conscious of his own sin and imperfection and suggesting that at least some of the evil from which he suffers is a price of the freedom which makes it possible for him to sin.

It is to be noted that in Hebraic religion the transcendent God is never an escape from the chaos of this world. This world is not meaningless and it is not necessary to escape from it to another supramundane world in order to preserve an ultimate optimism. For prophetic Judaism existence in this world is intensely meaningful, though the ultimate center of meaning transcends the world. It knows nothing of the distinction between pure form and concrete existence, or between a virtuous reason and a sinful body. It rejoices in the physical creation. "Lord, how manifold are thy works. In wisdom hast thou made them all." When the Psalmist faces the fact of death he does not have recourse to hope in immortality to save his optimism. He rather finds the glory of God exalted by the brevity of man. "For a thousand years in thy sight are but as yesterday when it is past and as a watch in the night." The threat of death to the meaning of life is destroyed by faith in a purpose which transcends the generations and by the thought that death is in some sense a just contribution for human evil. "For we are consumed by thine anger and by thy wrath we are troubled. Thou hast set our iniquities before thee and our secret sins in the light of thy countenance."

The prophetic religion from which Christianity took its rise is therefore not an other-worldly religion. It is thoroughly this-worldly, though it has nothing in common with the secularized this-worldliness of modern culture which finds meaning only in the historical process and knows nothing of a source of existence which transcends the process. Unfortunately, as this religion was philosophically elaborated in Greco-Roman thought it borrowed something from and was corrupted by Neo-Platonic dualism. Reason always has difficulty with an adequate view of transcendence and immanence. It inclines either to reduce it to a complete dualism or to a complete monism. As a result it expresses a world view which is either too pessimistic or too optimistic to do justice to all the facts of life. An adequate religion is always an ultimate optimism which has entertained all the facts which lead to pessimism. Its optimism is based upon a faith in a transcendent center of meaning which is never fully expressed in any partial value and is never exhausted in any concrete historical reality. But though it is not exhausted in any such reality it is incarnated there. Like the human personality in the human body, it lives in and through the body, but transcends it.

The other-worldliness of classical Christian orthodoxy came to a full expression in the Middle Ages. Though its sense of sin was sometimes morbid, and though it sometimes degenerated into a cult of death, it is not correct to attribute complete other-worldliness to the Middle Ages. Medieval Catholicism was sufficiently this-worldly to attempt the construction of a papal empire which would, through its universalism, transcend all the partial and parochial values of nationalism. It was sufficiently this-worldly even to give a religious sanction to the feudal structure of society, and to fall into the most grievous and the most perennial sin of religion: the sin of using the transcendent reference to absolutize rather than to criticize the partial achievements of history.

Our modern culture has acquired its most significant characteristics in its conscious and unconscious reaction to medieval culture. Its scientific discoveries made it impatient with the mythical errors of medieval religion. But it failed to realize that mythical descriptions of reality, though always inexact in describing detailed and historical fact, have the virtue of giving men a sense of depth in life. Pure science is always secular and horizontal in its references, and cannot express the vertical tendencies in culture which refer to the ultimate source of meaning in life. Modern culture substituted for the dualism and pessimism of medieval culture a simple naturalistic monism and optimism. It conceived history in dynamic terms and found it easy to identify change with progress, and to ascribe divine attributes to nature. It discovered in the "laws of nature" the very guarantee of the meaningfulness of the universe which it is the business of religion to find.

The religious attitude toward nature and its laws is evident in all of eighteenth-century literature. Holbach becomes religiously lyrical in addressing nature: "O Nature, sovereign of all being," he cries, "and ye her adorable daughters, virtue, reason, truth, remain forever our revered protectors. It is to you belong the praises of the human race." The identification of nature, virtue, reason and truth is a perfect example of the superficiality of this new mythology. The old mythology is sloughed off for being inexact, and a new mythology is created which is supposedly scientific but which ceases to be scientific as soon as it achieves mythical-religious proportions. Its laws are not laws at all, but projections of human ideals ("liberty, property and equality"). Its inability to discriminate between "nature as the entire system of things with the aggregate of all their properties" and "things as they would be without human intervention" (J. S. Mill) reveals that it has no recognition for the problem of depth and height in life. Human ideals are uncritically read into the natural process.

The religion of modern culture is in other words, a superficial religion which has discovered a meaningful world without having discovered the perils to meaning in death, sin and catastrophe. History has an immediate, an obvious, meaning because it spells progress. Progress is guaranteed by increasing intelligence because human sin is attributed to ignorance which will be removed by a proper pedagogy. It is surprising how little modern culture has qualified the optimism upon this point, first clearly stated by Condorcet. There is no recognition in it of the perils to anarchy which reside in human egoism, particularly collective egoism. The naturalistic optimism is revealed not only in its confidence in natural and rational processes, but in its identification of physical comfort with final bliss. Thus Priestley could declare: "Men will make their situation in the world abundantly more easy and comfortable; they will probably prolong their existence in it and grow daily more happy, each in himself, and more able and, I believe, more disposed to communicate happiness to others. Thus whatever the beginning of the world, the end will be paradisaical, beyond what our imaginations can conceive."* Thus an uncritical this-worldliness is substituted for the untenable other-worldliness of medievalism, and men become confused by a superficial optimism in the very moment when they celebrate their emancipation from a morbid pessimism.

Though there is a horde of moderns who still live by and in this kind of uncritical naturalism and optimism, it could not long claim the credulity of the more critical spirits. The simple identification of human ideals with the forces of nature inevitably gave way to a humanistic dualism in which a sharp distinction was drawn between the human and the natural world. No better definition of this dualism is given than that found in Huxley's famous Romanes lecture on Evolution and Ethics, in which he declared: "The cosmic process has no sort of relation to moral ends; the imitation of it by man is inconsistent with the first principles of ethics. . . . The ethical progress of society depends not on imitating the cosmic process, still less in running away from it, but in combating it." This kind of dualism is more realistic than the older type of naturalism, and it frees human moral life from slavish dependence upon the "laws of nature." Its general effect is to express optimism in terms of a human world of meaning and to relegate the world of nature to a realm of meaninglessness.

Thus the optimism of pure naturalism degenerates

*Essay on the First Principles of Government, p. 4.

into a fairly consistent pessimism, slightly relieved by a confidence in the meaningfulness of human life, even when its values must be maintained in defiance of nature's caprices. Bertrand Russell's now justly famous *Free Man's Worship* is a perfect and moving expression of this pessimism. "Brief and powerless is man's life. On him and all his race the slow sure doom sinks pitiless and dark. Blind to good and evil, omnipotent matter rolls on its relentless way. For man, condemned today to lose his dearest, tomorrow himself to pass through the gates of darkness, it remains only to cherish ere yet the blow falls, the lofty thoughts that ennoble his little day, proudly defiant of the irresistible forces which tolerate for a moment his knowledge and his condemnation, to sustain alone a weary and unyielding atlas, the world that his own ideals have fashioned despite the trampling march of unconscious power." It must be said in favor of this view that if human life and human ideals are the only source of meaning in existence, it is more realistic to regard the world of nature as a "trampling march of unconscious power" than to imagine that it exists only to support human purposes. In terms of realism sophisticated pessimism is preferable to the naïve optimism of the moderns.

Yet this pessimism is not completely realistic. The world of nature is after all not as inimical to the human enterprise as this view assumes. "Nature, the homely nurse, does all she can to make her foster child, her inmate man, forget the glories he has known and that imperial palace whence he came." The paradoxes of classical religion, in which God is known to be revealed in the beneficences of nature even though it is recognized that the processes of nature do not exhaust the final meaning of existence, are more realistic than this dualism. Furthermore, it leads to an unjustified human pride. Man celebrating himself as a "weary and unyielding atlas" is a slightly ludicrous object of worship. Inevitably this remnant of optmism finally yields to the prevailing pessimism until, as Joseph Wood Krutch confesses in his *Modern Temper*, "now we know that man is petty."

If anything further were required to complete the self-destruction of modern optimism we have it in the tragic events of modern history. They have negated practically every presupposition upon which modern culture was built. History does not move forward without catastrophe, happiness is not guaranteed by the multiplication of physical comforts, social harmony is not easily created by more intelligence, and human nature is not as good or as harmless as had been supposed. We are thus living in a period in which either the optimism of yesterday has given way to despair, or in which some of the less sophisticated moderns try desperately to avoid the abyss of despair by holding to credos which all of the facts have disproved.

15

OPTIMISM, PESSIMISM AND

RELIGIOUS FAITH—II

Long before the disintegration of modern optimism the liberal culture in which it lies embedded was challenged by a new mythology which grew out of the experiences of those who had been disinherited by the injustices of modern industrial civilization, and who therefore knew from their own experience that the liberal picture of human nature and human history was not true. The Marxian mythology, whatever its ultimate optimism, is thoroughgoing in its pessimism when it analyzes the facts of contemporary history and of human nature in the contemporary environment. Human ideals are but the rationalizations of human interest. And human history is a series of class conflicts between people of varying and contradictory interests. This series of conflicts will end in the final destruction of our present social system.

In this Marxian mythology some of the old paradoxes of Jewish mythology reappear. Marx gives us a secularized version of Jewish prophecy, though it is not nearly as secularized as the liberal mythology. Its view of history is less simple, and its view of human nature is more true, than that of liberalism. Though it denies God as the center and source of life's meaning more explicitly than liberal naturalism, it implicitly avows a divine support for human purposes, more particularly for the very specific purposes of those who intend to guide history toward a classless society. In the words of Max Eastman, the Marxian world "is made of matter, but this matter performs the essential functions of spirit, that of going where the believer wants it to go by a 'self-active' dialectical movement which constitutes its 'essence.'" Here we have again the Jewish hope for a redeemed world, not above history but at the end of history. Here also is the idea of the Jewish prophets that history is constituted of the judgments as well as the mercies of God. The provisional pessimism is relieved by various types of optimistic faith and hope.

The chaos of the moment does not drive the Marxian to despair as it does the disappointed liberal. He sees meaning in this chaos, as the Jewish prophets of the exile discovered meaning in the vicissitudes of their nation. God uses the wrath of man to praise him, and the destruction of capitalism is but the necessary prelude to the construction of an ideal society. In some of its aspects the Marxian mythology of history is a profoundly religious one. For it, life is not a simple harmony but a chaos which has the possibilities of harmony within it. Human nature is not immediately good, but it contains potentialities for co-operative living under the proper environment. In other respects the Marxian mythology is quite primitive, however, and in others, again, it is too much the child of secular modernism to escape its errors of superficiality.

It is primitive in its glorification of a particular social group. The Marxian conception of a Messianic class is a kind of primitive totemism. There are, of course, solid justifications for regarding the victims of injustice in modern society as a fateful class. Experience has given them eyes to see what keener eyes do not see. Nevertheless, the Marxian identification of the fate of a class with the future of civilization itself is akin to the pre-prophetic messianism of Judaism; and it is not dissimilar to the modern tribalism, propagated, for instance, by the Nazis. I do not mean to imply that it is not more legitimate to ascribe universal values to the objectives of the working class than to endow a particular (Aryan) race with divine significance. Nevertheless, in each case the individual rescues life from meaninglessness by attachment and religious loyalty to a partial human community.

The religious significance of this type of optimism is clearly revealed in an article by Rebecca Pitts in *The New Masses** in which it is declared: "The loss of religious faith is good only if we can put in its place a faith in life so real and driving that it endows men's acts with an equal validity. . . . Of course there is only one solution—the solution which the bourgeoisie rejects as worse than the total annihilation of modern society. . . . Men become sincere and incorruptible as they identify their aims with those of the working class as a whole." This is a new kind of patriotism, and one may well believe that it has possibilities which the older patriotic loyalties lacked. It will contribute more to the destruction of an unjust social system and the building of a new one than the loyalties which express themselves in futile conflicts between various races and nations. But it is not free of the demonic pretensions which express themselves whenever a partial human value is given absolute significance by religious emotion. If it should be finally proved, as well it may, that the working class is an important but not a sole instrument of a new society, the optimism of those whose whole universe

*"Something To Believe In," *The New Masses*, March 13, 1934.

of meaning is contained in the life of one class will degenerate into pessimism again.

Perhaps more important than the primitivism of Marxian religion is its secularized naturalism. Its high ideals of a just society are to be completely realized in history. It does not see that the highest ideals of justice, love and brotherhood are concepts of the human spirit when spirit completely transcends the infirmities of the flesh and the frustrations of history. They must be approximated but they will never be fully realized. Marxianism is, in short, another form of utopianism. We have had utopian solutions to the problem of pessimism throughout history. They point to a future when the chaos of the world will be overcome and life will become a complete harmony and a fulfilled meaning. They save optimism not by faith but by hope. Life is not regarded as meaningful as it exists, with all its sad disappointments; but significance is imparted to it by what it will be.

There is an element of truth in this utopianism, as there is truth in every sober hope. Some of the chaos of human existence can be overcome. It is possible to have a society in which there will be security for every one rather than insecurity for the many. No doubt the proper education and experience can reduce human egoism and can beguile it into less socially harmful expressions. But this kingdom of God upon earth where every one will give according to his ability and take according to his need, this anarchistic millennium of communist dreams, what is that but a confused naturalistic version of a religious hope? The optimism which is based upon it may outlast one five-year plan and possibly two or three. But after many five-year plans have come and gone and it is discovered that strong men still tend to exploit the weak, and that shrewd men still take advantage of the simple, and that no society can guarantee the satisfaction of all legitimate desires, and that no social arrangement is proof against the misery which we bring upon each other by our sin, what will become of this optimism? We might have a society in which greed is practically abolished, and yet men would suffer from injustice in such a society, as, for instance, some monks suffered from the cruel tyranny of their abbots in the monasteries of the Middle Ages.

An optimism which depends upon the hope of the complete realization of our highest ideals in history is bound to suffer ultimate disillusionment. All such optimistic illusions have resulted in such a fate throughout history. Always there comes a period when scoffers will arise to say, "Since the fathers have fallen asleep, all things continue as they were from the beginning of creation" (2 Peter 3:4). The beauty and meaning of human life are partially revealed in ideals and aspirations which transcend all possibilities of achievement in history. They may be approximated and each approximation may lead to further visions. But the hope of their complete fulfillment arises from a confusion of spirit and nature, and a failure to realize that life in each moment of history moves not only forward but upward, and that the vertical movement must be expressed no matter how far the horizontal movement on the plane of history is carried. Marxism may represent a more realistic politics than eighteenth-century democratic idealism. But as a religion it will end just where the latter ended. Its optimism will sink ultimately into despair.

The optimism of historic Hebraism and of classical Christianity (except where the latter has been vitiated by a too thorough dualism) is much more robust and satisfying than the modern substitutes which have run their course. While modern optimism was in its prime it could sneer at the pessimism of historic religion because the illusions of the former prevented it from recognizing the tragic realities of life and history which the latter had incorporated into its universe of meaning. Now that these illusions have been dispelled, it is possible to recognize again that historic religion has a note of provisional pessimism in its optimism, for the simple reason that it takes cognizance of more of the facts of human existence.

The view of life and the world in classical religion of the Jewish and Christian tradition can be stated in rough outline, though it is impossible in such an

outline to do justice to the differences and contradictions which have appeared in the long history of
Jewish and Christian thought. In this view human
life is meaningful even though its existence in a world
of nature, which is not completely sympathetic to the
human enterprise, is not fully explained. The world
of nature is not completely interpreted in terms of
human values or ideals, as in naïve naturalism, nor is
it simply a dark abyss or a "trampling march of unconscious power" which man defies and against which
he rebels. Man and nature are reconciled by faith in
a center and source of meaning which transcends both
man and nature.

It is not assumed that God's purposes can be fully
measured by any measuring rod of human ideals. In
one of the greatest books of religious poetry, the book
of Job, man questions the justice of God in terms of
human standards, but is finally overwhelmed by the
majesty and mystery of existence, and Job confesses
contritely, "I have uttered that I understood not;
things too wonderful for me which I knew not—
wherefore I abhor myself and repent in dust and
ashes."* Something of that idea, *i.e.*, that the world
is intensely meaningful, even though its meaning
transcends human comprehension, runs as one strain
through all profound religion. "To know that there
is meaning but not to know the meaning," declares

*Job, 42:6.

the modern J. Middleton Murry, "that is bliss." That word is in the spirit of classical religion. It expresses a trust in life even when the immediate facts of life seem to outrage our conception of what life ought to be. "Though he slay me yet will I trust him."

The transcendent God, most adequately pictured in the mythos of a creator God, is, though clothed in mystery, not the God of deism. His purposes are relevant and related to the human enterprise, and the highest human virtues give us some glimpses of His purposes. He is a God of justice and love. His majesty is no more certain than His moral perfection. The difficulty of bringing God's omnipotence into consistent relation with his goodness has engaged all ages of religious thought. But the most adequate religion solves its problems in paradoxes rather than schemes of consistency, and has never wavered in believing that God is both the ground of our existence and the ultimate pinnacle of perfection toward which existence tends. Therefore, the highest human excellencies are clues to the character of God.

Faith in a moral perfection which transcends human perfection is the basis of the note of contrition in all great religion. Man does not feel himself an outraged innocent in the evil world. Indeed, he accepts some of the evil which befalls him in the world as a just punishment for his sin. While traditional religion usually overstates the case at this point and makes human sin responsible for all the imperfections of nature, it remains true nevertheless that this insight actually incorporates a good deal of what might be regarded as chaos into the universe of meaning.

It can be seen that love is the law of life, even when people do not live by the law of love. When that law is broken the consequences are death and destruction. For the religious man the tortures and agonies through which our generation is going and through which other generations will probably go, represent the inevitable judgment upon a civilization which violated the law of brotherhood and has destroyed itself by these violations. Chaos and death may suggest meaninglessness to the proud man, but to the contrite man they are revelations of the consequences of human sin; and if they cannot be completely comprehended in those terms they may still be regarded as a part of the meaning of life which has not been fully disclosed to man. They may thus be accepted with gratitude, and the believer is able to say, "The Lord hath given, the Lord hath taken away, praised be the name of the Lord," or, in the words of Francis of Assisi, "Praised be my Lord for our sister the death of the body from which no man escapeth."

To believe in a meaningful existence which has its center and source beyond itself makes it possible to preserve moral vitality, because the world as it exists is not regarded as perfect even though it is meaningful. Hebraic thought has always had greater ethical vigor than that of the Greeks; and Christian thought, where it has been most vital ethically, has borrowed heavily from Jewish thought. Purely rationalistic interpretations of life and existence easily make one of two mistakes. They either result in idealistic or pantheistic sanctifications of historic reality, in which the given is appreciated too uncritically to allow for a protest against its imperfections, or they degenerate into dualism, in which the world of concrete reality is relegated to the realm of the unredeemed and unredeemable. In the best Jewish-Christian thought, which conceives of God as both the creator and the judge of the world, evil must be overcome even while it is recognized that evil is part of the inevitable mystery of existence. There is no disposition to declare that all "partial evil is universal good." In fact there is always a devil in classical religious mythology, and the devil is a symbol of the belief that evil is regarded as an actual rebellion against God. Of course this realism is always balanced by an ultimate optimism, because it is never believed that the devil can seriously threaten the rule of God.

There have been times when Christian orthodoxy was too dualistic and pessimistic to take the moral and social tasks of society seriously. Against its complete pessimism the thought of the eighteenth century and of modernity in general was a necessary corrective. But it must never be forgotten that the pessimism against which modernity rebelled was but a corruption of a world view which was critical of the moral achievements of historic man because it viewed them from a high perspective. Only in a religion in which there is a true sense of transcendence can we find the resource to convict every historical achievement of incompleteness, and to prevent the sanctification of the relative values of any age or any era.

The qualified optimism of an adequate religion will never satisfy the immature minds who have found some superficial harmony in the world in which the evils and threats to meaning are not taken into account. Nor will it satisfy those who think that every ill from which man suffers can be eliminated in some proximate future. It will nerve men to exhaust all their resources in building a better world, in overcoming human strife, in mitigating the fury of man's injustice to man, and in establishing a society in which some minimal security for all can be achieved. But in an adequate religion there will be a recognition of the fact that nothing accomplished along the horizontal line of history can eliminate the depth of life which is revealed at every point of history. Let man stand at any point in history, even in a society which has realized his present dreams of justice, and if he surveys the human problem profoundly he will see that every perfection which he has achieved points beyond itself to a greater perfection, and that this greater perfection throws light upon his sins and imperfections. He will feel in that tension between what is and what ought to be the very glory of life, and will come to know that the perfection which eludes him is not only a human possibility and impossibility, but a divine fact.

"Religion," declares Whitehead, "is a vision of something which stands beyond, behind and within the passing flux of things, something which is real and yet waiting to be realized; something which is a remote possibility and yet the greatest of present facts; something that gives meaning to all that passes and yet eludes apprehension; something whose possession is the final good and yet is beyond all reach; something which is the ultimate ideal and yet the hopeless quest."* These paradoxes are in the spirit of great religion. The mystery of life is comprehended in meaning, though no human statement of the meaning can fully resolve the mystery. The tragedy of life is recognized, but faith prevents tragedy from being pure tragedy. Perplexity remains, but there is no perplexity unto despair. Evil is neither accepted as inevitable nor regarded as a proof of the meaninglessness of life.

*A. N. Whitehead, *Science and the Modern World*, p. 267.

Gratitude and contrition are mingled, which means that life is both appreciated and challenged. To such faith the generations are bound to return after they have pursued the mirages in the desert to which they are tempted from time to time by the illusions of particular eras.

16

THE CHRISTIAN CHURCH IN
A SECULAR AGE*

F OR THE PAST TWO HUN-
dred years the Christian Church has been proclaiming
its gospel in a world which no longer accepted the essentials of the Christian Faith. The Western world,
particularly the more advanced industrial nations, has
come increasingly under the sway of what has been
called a secular culture. Secularism is most succinctly
defined as the explicit disavowal of the sacred. The
holy in every religion is that reality upon which all
things depend, in terms of which they are explained
and by which they are judged. It is the ultimate mystery, but also the ultimate source of all meaning. For
the Christian Faith holiness is ascribed only to the

*Delivered before Oxford Conference on Church and Com-
munity in 1937.

God who is the Creator, Judge and Redeemer of the world. The world is made and sustained by Him. Its historical realities are thus the fruits of His creative will. The world is judged by Him. Its sins stand under His divine judgment. The world is redeemed by Him. Without His grace mediated through Christ, human existence remains a problem to itself, being unable to escape by any effort of its own from the contradictions of a sinful existence.

THE RELIGION OF SECULARISM

In contrast to this faith, modern secularism has been interpreted by the Christian Church too much in terms of secularism's own disavowal of religious faith. Strictly speaking, there is no such thing as secularism. An explicit denial of the sacred always contains some implied affirmation of a holy sphere. Every explanation of the meaning of human existence must avail itself of some principle of explanation which cannot be explained. Every estimate of values involves some criterion of value which cannot be arrived at empirically. Consequently the avowedly secular culture of today turns out upon close examination to be either a pantheistic religion which identifies existence in its totality with holiness, or a rationalistic humanism for which human reason is essentially god or a vitalistic humanism which worships some unique or particular vital force in the individual or the community as its god, that is, as the object of its unconditioned loyalty.

This latter faith, the product of the romantic movement in western civilization, is the most obvious form of idolatry. It is also the most explicitly religious. Its emergence, particularly on the European Continent, in these latter days of a dying bourgeois culture, proves the irrelevance of critical categories which imply a simple and unqualified contrast between the religious and the secular. There are no irreligious cultures; and if there were, it could not be assumed that a religious culture is intrinsically superior to an irreligious one. The question is not whether we worship a god. That is not the question, on the one hand, because all men do, whether implicitly or explicitly; and on the other hand, the worship of false gods is in no sense preferable to complete agnosticism, if the latter were possible.

The civilization and culture in which we are called upon to preach the Christian gospel is, in other words, not irreligious, but a devotee of a very old religion, dressed in a new form. It is the old religion of self-glorification. This is a very old religion because it involves the quintessence of human sin, as defined by St. Paul in the first chapter of Romans. Speaking of the Gentiles and their culpability in the sight of God he declares: "So that they are without excuse: because that, when they knew God, they glorified Him not as God, neither were thankful; but became vain in their imaginations, and their foolish heart was darkened. Professing themselves to be wise, they became fools [and what an accurate description that is of the vainglory of our modern era], and changed the glory of the uncorruptible God into an image made like to corruptible man, and to birds and four-footed beasts, and creeping things."

Every form of modern secularism contains an implicit or explicit self-glorification and deification in the sense described in the Letter to the Romans. Humanistic rationalism, forgetting that human reason as well as human physical existence is a derived, dependent, created and finite reality, makes it into a principle of interpretation of the meaning of life; and believes that its gradual extension is the guarantee of the ultimate destruction of evil in history. It mistakes the image of God in man for God Himself. It does not realize that the freedom by which man is endowed in his rational nature is the occasion for his sin as well as the ground of morality. It does not understand that by this reason nature's harmless will-to-live is transmuted into a sinful will-to-power. It is by this reason that men make pretentious claims for their partial and relative insights, falsely identifying them with absolute truth. Thus rationalism always involves itself in two descending scales of self-deification. What begins as the deification of humanity in abstract terms ends as the deification of a particular type of man, who supposedly possesses ultimate insights. In Aristotelian rationalism this latter development is expressed in the deification of the aristocrat, whom to glorify the slave exists. In modern rationalism the final result is a glorification of bourgeois perspectives.

The recent emergence of a more explicit type of self-glorification in race, State and nation, in religions of *Blut und Boden* represents the victory of romanticism over rationalism, to speak in purely cultural terms. More profoundly considered, this romantic development is a cynical reaction to the hypocritical pretensions of the rationalists. Let those of us who live in such parts of Western civilization in which the old rational humanism and universalism is not yet completely disintegrated guard ourselves against premature self-righteous judgments. It may be that our type of humanism represents a more sincere attempt to establish universal values and expresses an honest devotion to European civilization rather than to the defiant strength of a particular nation. But on the other hand, this bourgeois humanism tends to be oblivious to its own partial, national and bourgeois perspectives. Having erroneously identified its truth with the eternal truth, it naturally elicits the reaction of a curious kind of cynical romanticism. It is not without significance that rational humanism is still most robust in the nations which hold a dominant position, politically and economically, in the Western world, more particularly the Anglo-Saxon nations; while what we abhor as primitivistic romanticism flourishes in the less satisfied nations. Hypocrisy and implicit or covert self-glorification are always the particular temptation of the victors; and cynicism and a more explicit self-glorification the sin of the vanquished. The necessity of compensating for outraged self-esteem is the cause of this greater degree of explicitness in the deification of self.

The whole story of modern culture might be truly chronicled in terms of the Parable of the Prodigal Son. The more rationalistic humanism is the son in the first stages of his emancipation from his father. The temper of modern culture is expressed quite precisely in the words of the son: "Father, give me the portion of goods that falleth to me." Our civilization did not want to recognize its dependence upon a divine father, who is the source of all life and the judge of all human actions. It wanted an autonomous culture. It separated the "goods that falleth to me" from the divine patrimony and forgot the dangers of anarchy in this independence. The more romantic type of modern humanism, as revealed in the religio-political movements of the Continent, represent a more advanced state of disintegration. Here the son is "wasting his substance in riotous living," a civilization allowing the vital energies of peoples and nations to express themselves in anarchic conflict with one another, and insisting that any vital or unique energy is morally self-justifying. The "mighty famine" when the son begins to be in want is still in the future, but our civilization is destined for such a catastrophe as so certain a consequence of the anarchy of its conflicting national passions and ambitions, that one may well speak of it as part of the contemporary picture.

To leave for a moment the Parable of the Prodigal Son, a further reaction to bourgeois rationalism and humanism must be recorded which seeks to eliminate the errors of this dominant form of secularism. I refer to Marxism and the revolt of the proletarians in the Western world against the privileged sections of the community. In this newer form of humanism there is an explicit recognition of the finiteness of the human mind and the relation of human ideals to human interests; to the sinfulness, in short, of all human culture. Yet this very philosophy which sees the pretensions of all "the wise, the mighty and the noble" so clearly insists that it will be able to arrive at an absolute and universal position. In this creed the life of the proletariat has some mystic union with the absolute.

Here then we have a nice combination of the romantic and the rationalistic strains in modern culture, a glorification of the vitality of the burden bearers of the world as the instrument of an ultimate universalistic humanism; but no recognition that this fateful class is also composed of sinful men and that their sin will become more apparent as soon as they cease to be the oppressed and become the victors. Inasfar as Marxism seeks to establish genuinely universal values it must not be equated with the fascism which defies every common interest in the name of its own self-justifying vitality. Nor can its superiority over the pretentious rationalism of bourgeois life be denied. But unfortunately, as every culture which is not confronted with the one holy God, the Creator, Lord and Judge of the world, it also ends in the sin of self-glorification.

THE MESSAGE OF REPENTANCE

The question is, what shall the Christian Church say to this modern culture, which began its adventure in autonomy with such gay self-assurance, which is already so deeply involved in "riotous living" and which faces so certain a doom of a mighty famine?

We must, of course, preach the gospel to this, as to every generation. Our gospel is one which assures salvation in the Cross of Christ to those who heartily repent of their sins. It is a gospel of the Cross; and the Cross is a revelation of the love of God only to those who have first stood under it as a judgment. It is in the Cross that the exceeding sinfulness of human sin is revealed. It is in the Cross that we become conscious how, not only what is worst, but what is best in human culture and civilization is involved in man's rebellion against God. It was Roman law, the pride of all pagan civilization, and Hebraic religion, the acme of religious devotion, which crucified the Lord. Thus does the Cross reveal the problem of all human culture and the dilemma of every human civilization.

Repentance is the first key into the door of the Kingdom of God. God resisteth the proud and giveth grace to the humble. Whenever men trust their own righteousness, their own achievements, whenever they interpret the meaning of life in terms of the truth in their own culture or find in their own capacities a sufficient steppingstone to the Holy and the Divine, they rest their life upon a frail reed which inevitably breaks and leaves their life meaningless.

Perhaps that is why the truest interpretations of the Christian faith have come in moments of history when civilizations were crumbling and the processes of history and the judgments of God had humbled human arrogance. The faith of the Hebrew prophets was thus formulated when the culture religion of Israel was threatened and finally overcome by the mighty civilizations of Assyria and Babylon. Augustine wrote the *City of God* when Roman civilization, once mighty enough to seem identical with civilization itself, had become the helpless victim of barbarians; and the renewal of the Christian gospel in the Protestant Reformation was, historically speaking, the consequence as well as the cause of the crumbling of a once proud medieval civilization. Proud men and successful civilizations find it difficult to know God, because they are particularly tempted to make themselves God. That is why "not many mighty, not many noble, not many wise after the flesh are called." Without the godly sorrow that worketh repentance there can be no salvation.

THE MESSAGE OF HOPE

Just as the Christian gospel calls the proud to repent, it assures those who despair of a new hope. It is interesting how every religion which imparts a superficial meaning to life, and grounds that meaning in a dubious sanctity, finally issues in despair. Those who make the family their god must despair when the family is proved to be only a little less mortal than the individual. Those who make a god of their nation must despair when the might of their nation crumbles, as every creaturely and sinful might must: "For we are consumed by thine anger and by thy wrath are we troubled." That is the despair which awaits many a young nationalistic pagan of Europe today. They might even, if they could see truly, despair in the triumph of their nation, for the nation in triumph is less worthy of reverence than the nation in defeat. Pride accentuates its sins, and there are no sufferings to prompt pity as a handmaiden of love in the heart of the patriot.

Every humanistic creed is a cosmos of meaning sustained by a thin ice on the abysmal deeps of meaninglessness and chaos. Only the faith in God, who has been "our dwelling place in all generations," and who was God "before the mountains were brought forth or ever the earth and the world were made," can survive the vicissitudes of history, can rescue human existence from the despair in which it is periodically involved by its sinful pretensions, and the tragic disappointment of its facile hopes.

The fulfillment of life, according to our Christian faith, is possible only through the mercy of God. All superficial questions about the meaning of life, all simple religions which imagine that faith in any god is better than no faith at all, fail to recognize that the ultimate question is not whether life has a meaning (which it must have or no one could live), but whether or not the meaning is tragic. The only serious competitor to Christianity as a spiritual religion is Buddhism, and in Buddhism life is conceived in terms of pure tragedy. Christianity is a faith which takes us through tragedy to beyond tragedy, by way of the Cross to a victory in the Cross. The God whom we worship takes the contradictions of human existence into Himself. This knowledge is a stumbling block to the Jews, and to the Gentiles foolishness, but to

them that are called it is the power and the wisdom
of God. This is a wisdom beyond human knowledge,
but not contrary to human experience. Once known,
the truth of the gospel explains our experiences which
remain inexplicable on any other level. Through it we
are able to understand life in all of its beauty and its
terror, without being beguiled by its beauty or driven
to despair by its terror.

NOT OF THE WORLD, BUT IN THE WORLD

While the gospel which we preach reveals a world
which in its ground and its fulfillment transcends
human history, it does not abstract us from this present history with all of its conflicts and tragic disappointments of arrogant hopes. We are in the world,
and God's Will, His Judgment and His Mercy im-
pinge upon our daily actions and historic problems.
We must bring forth fruits meet for repentance.
What can those fruits be but the fruits of "love, joy,
peace?" When the Church proclaims the love commandment to the world as the law of God it must
guard against the superficial moralism of telling the
world that it can save itself if men will only stop
being selfish and learn to be loving. We dare not
forget that in us, as well as in those who do not acknowledge the Christian gospel, there is a law in our
members that wars against the law that is in our mind.
The law of love is not kept simply by being preached.

Yet it is the law of life and must be both preached and practised. It is a terrible heresy to suggest that, because the world is sinful, we have a right to construct a Machiavellian politics or a Darwinian sociology as normative for Christians.

What is significant about the Christian ethic is precisely this: that it does not regard the historic as normative. Man may be, as Thomas Hobbes observed, a wolf to his fellowman. But this is not his essential nature. Let Christianity beware, particularly radical Protestantism, that it does not accept the habits of a sinful world as the norms of a Christian collective life. For the Christian only the law of love is normative. He would do well to remember that he is a sinner who has never perfectly kept the law of God. But neither must he forget that he is a child of God who stands under that law. Much of what passes for theological profundity today is no more than a subtle re-enactment of the part of the son in the Lord's Parable who promised to do the father's will and did not, leaving his will to be done by the son who had refused to promise it. How accurately that little parable of Christ pictures the superior passion for human justice of many outside the Church as against those who are in it. Frequently, believing Christians are tempted by their recognition of the sinfulness of human existence to disavow their own responsibility for a tolerable justice in the world's affairs. Justice is not love.

Justice presupposes the conflict of life with life and seeks to mitigate it. Every relative justice therefore stands under the judgment of the law of love, but it is also an approximation of it.

A Christian pessimism which becomes a temptation to irresponsibility toward all those social tasks which constantly confront the life of men and nations, tasks of ordering the productive labor of men, of adjudicating their conflicts, of arbitrating their divergent desires, of raising the level of their social imagination and increasing the range of their social sympathies, such a pessimism cannot speak redemptively to a world constantly threatened by anarchy and suffering from injustice. The Christian gospel which transcends all particular and contemporary social situations can be preached with power only by a Church which bears its share of the burdens of immediate situations in which men are involved, burdens of establishing peace, of achieving justice, and of perfecting justice in the spirit of love. Thus is the Kingdom of God which is not of this world made relevant to every problem of the world.

THE DANGER OF PROFANIZATION

If the problem of presenting the Christian ethic to a non-Christian world without the spirit of self-righteousness is difficult, an even more far-reaching problem is the presentation of the gospel to a secu-

216

lar age. The truths of the Christian gospel are sim-ple and clear. But it is not easy for any human insti-tution to mediate them without pride or hypocrisy; and the Church is a human institution, though it is that institution where it is known that all human life stands under a divine judgment and within a divine mercy. The real difficulty of preaching the gospel of God's mercy to the prodigal son, our modern culture, lies in the temptation to play the part of the elder brother in the Lord's Parable. One might indeed elab-orate this Parable without disloyalty to its meaning, with the suggestion that the younger son might well have been prompted to leave his father's house be-cause of the insufferable self-righteousness of the elder brother. At any rate, it is quite obvious that no Christian Church has a right to preach to a so-called secular age without a contrite recognition of the short-comings of historic Christianity which tempted the modern age to disavow its Christian faith.

Secularism is, on the one hand, the expression of man's sinful self-sufficiency. It may be, on the other hand, a reaction to profanity. Some men are atheists because of a higher implicit theism than that professed by believers. They reject God because His name has been taken in vain, and they are unable to distinguish between His Holiness and its profanization. It is popular today in Christian circles to speak somewhat contemptuously of the errors and illusions of the secular culture which challenged Christianity so optimistically in the last two centuries and finds itself in such confusion today. It would be well to remember, however, that the primary conscious motive of this secularism (whatever may have been its unconscious and more sinful motives) was to break the chains which a profane Christianity had placed upon man.

A profane Christianity, like the elder brother, ostensibly maintains its sense of dependence upon the Father, but it uses this relationship to satisfy a sinful egotism. It falsely identifies its relative and partial human insights with God's wisdom, and its partial and relative human achievements with God's justice. A profane Christianity falsely identifies the Church with the Kingdom of God. Since the historic Church is always touched with human finiteness, is subject to sociological forces and pressures, and victim of the prejudices and illusions of particular ages, any tendency to obscure or deny this fact becomes the final and most terrible expression of human sinfulness. Of that sin no Church has been free.

Protestants may believe, and not without a measure of truth, that this sin of profaning the Holiness of God, of using His Name in vain, is a particular danger in Catholicism, for Catholicism has a doctrine of the Church in which what is human and what is divine in the Church is constantly subject to a confused identification of the one with the other. Yet no historic

Christian institution is free of this sin. Every vehicle of God's grace, the preacher of the word, the prince of the Church, the teacher of theology, the historic institution, the written word, the sacred canon, all these are in danger of being revered as if they were themselves divine. The aura of the divine word, which is transmitted through them, falsely covers their human frailties. The Christian Church has never followed St. Paul rigorously enough in his disavowal of divinity: "And when the people saw what Paul had done they lifted up their voices saying, in the speech of Lyconia: The gods have come down to us in the likeness of men . . . which when the Apostles Paul and Barnabas heard of they rent their clothes and ran in among the people crying out and saying, Sirs, why do ye these things? We also are men of like passions with you and preach unto you, that ye should turn from these vanities unto the living God, which made heaven and earth and the sea and all things that are therein" (Acts 14:11–15).

SECULARISM AS A REACTION AGAINST A PROFANE CHRISTIANITY

Modern secularism was forced to resist a profanization of the holiness of God both in the realm of the truth and in the realm of the good, in both culture and ethics. In the realm of culture the Christian religion was tempted to complete the incompleteness of all human culture by authoritative dicta, supposedly drawn from Scripture. It forgot that theology is a human discipline subject to the same relativities as any other human discipline. If modern culture was wrong in regarding the Anselmic axiom *"Credo ut intelligam"* as absurd because it failed to understand that reason cannot function without the presuppositions of faith, Christian culture was wrong in insinuating the specific insights and prejudices of a particular age into the *"credo."* While modern science was wrong in assuming that its descriptions of detailed historical sequences in nature and history offered an adequate insight into the meaning of life, Christian culture was wrong in regarding its knowledge of the transhistorical sources of the meaning of life as adequate explanations of detailed sequences and efficient causation.

Thus we have been subjected for centuries to a conflict between a theology which had become a bad science, and a science which implied an unconscious theology, a theology of unconscious presuppositions about the ultimate meaning of life. These presuppositions were doubly wrong. They were wrong in content and erroneous in being implicit rather than explicit. But surely the responsibility for this confusing conflict rests as much with a theology which had become a bad science as with a science which is a bad theology. In one sense all Orthodox Christian theology has been guilty of the sin of profanity. It has insisted on the literal and historic truth of its myths, forgetting that it is the function and character of religious myth to speak of the eternal in relation to time, and that it cannot therefore be a statement of temporal sequences.

No Christian theology, worthy of its name, can therefore be without gratitude to the forces of modern secularism inasfar as their passion for truth was a passion for God. They failed indeed to recognize that every search for truth begins with a presupposition of faith. They did not know for this reason how vulnerable they were to the sneer of Pilate: "What is truth?"; and they could not consequently appreciate the affirmation of Christ: "I am the truth." But this secularization of truth is no more culpable than the religious profanization of truth which blandly appropriates the truth in Christ for every human vagary and prejudice, for every relative insight and temporal perspective.

The profanity of historic Christianity in regard to the problem of righteousness has been even more grievous than in regard to the problem of truth. Every human civilization is a compromise between the necessities and contingencies of nature and the Kingdom of God with its absolute love commandment. This is as true of a Christian as of an unchristian civilization. In a Christian, as well as in an unchristian civilization, the strong are tempted to exploit the weak, the community is tempted to regard itself as an end in itself, and the rulers are tempted to use their power for their own advantage. When the welter of relative justice and injustice, which emerges out of this conflict and confluence of forces, is falsely covered with the aura of the divine, and when the preservation of such a civilization is falsely enjoined as a holy duty, and when its rebels and enemies are falsely regarded as enemies of God, it is only natural that those who are most conscious of the injustices of a given social order, because they suffer from them, should adopt an attitude of cynical secularism toward the pretensions of sanctity made in behalf of a civilization. A profanization of the holiness of God leads inevitably to an effort to eliminate the sacred from human life. Invariably this effort is partially informed by a covert and implicit sense of the sacred, morally higher than the historic sanctity against which it protests. One need only study the perverted religious intensity of the nineteenth-century Russian nihilists to understand how a warfare against God may be prompted by a prophetic passion for God and scorn for the dubious political divinities which seek to borrow His holiness.

It is impossible to understand the secularism of either the commercial classes or the radical proletarians of the past hundred and fifty years if it is not appreciated to what degree this secularism represents a reaction to the too intimate and organic relation of Christianity with a feudal society. The priest of religion and the landlord of an agrarian society were too closely related to each other and the former was too frequently the apologist and auxiliary gendarme of the latter.

It may seem that this charge falls more heavily upon Catholicism than upon Protestantism, not only because of the historic relation of the former with a medieval culture and feudal civilization, but also because the latter is less prone to identify itself with the detailed economic and political arrangements of any society. But with its higher degree of detachment Protestantism has sometimes also revealed a higher degree of social irresponsibility. It has allowed its pessimism to betray it into a negative sanctification of a given social order on the assumption that any given order is preferable to anarchy and that the disturbance of the *status quo* might lead to anarchy.

Thus Catholicism and Protestantism, between them, have exhausted the possibilities of error in Christianity's relation to society. In either case peace and order through power were estimated too highly and the inevitable injustice of every stabilization of power was judged too leniently. Frequently Christianity was content to regard deeds of personal generosity and charity as adequate expressions of the Christian love commandment within a civilization in which every basic

223

relationship was a complete denial of that commandment.

The secularism both of our modern bourgeois civilization and of the more proletarian civilizations which threaten to replace it, is therefore something more than the religion of self-glorification. It combines this sin with a passion for justice which frequently puts the historic Church to shame. If the Christian Church is to preach its gospel effectively to men of such a culture, it must understand the baffling mixture of a new profanity and resistance to an old profanity which is comprehended in this culture.

JUDGMENT MUST BEGIN AT THE HOUSE OF GOD

Such a recognition is the clue to the problem of an effective proclamation of the Christian gospel in our day. If we preach repentance, it must be repentance for those who accept the Lord as well as for those who pretend to deny Him. If we preach the judgment of God upon a sinful world, it must be judgment upon us as well as upon those who do not acknowledge His judgments. If we preach the mercy of God, it must be with a humble recognition that we are in need of it as much as those who do not know God's mercy in Christ. If we preach the obligation of the love commandment, the preacher must know that he violates that commandment as well as those who do not consciously accept its obligation. Nothing is cheaper and more futile than the preaching of a simple moralism which is based upon the assumption that the world need only to be told that selfishness is sin and that love is the law of life to beguile it from the anarchy of sin in which it is at present engulfed. Such a moralism, to which the modern Church is particularly prone, is blind to the real tragedy and persistence of sin in the world.

To preach to others and become ourselves castaways is a peril in which all holy business is done. It is a peril to which the Church must succumb if it does not constantly hear the challenge of God to Jeremiah to "separate the precious from the vile"; to distinguish between what is genuinely the Lord's will and our will, His holiness and our sin in the work of the Christian Church. The Kingdom of God was ushered in by the preaching of John the Baptist. The most profound element in John's message of repentance was expressed in the words, "And think not to say within yourselves, We have Abraham to our Father; for I say unto you that God is able of these stones to raise up children unto Abraham."* Not only the racial inheritors of a divine promise are tempted to rest complacently in the assurance "We have Abraham to our Father." That is a temptation which assails all inheritors of a divine promise, including the Christian Church, the "Israel of God." It is wholesome there-

*Matt. 3:9.

fore for the Church to stand under the stinging rebuke "God is able of these stones to raise up children unto Abraham," a rebuke in the form of a statement of fact which history has validated again and again.

If the conscience of the Church feels the relevance to its own life of that rebuke, it can preach the gospel of a holy God, holy in righteousness and in mercy, without making sinful claims for itself in the name of that holiness, and it will be able to speak to the conscience of this generation, rebuking its sins without assuming a role of self-righteousness and overcoming its despair without finding satisfaction in the sad disillusionment into which the high hopes of modernity have issued.

226

DATE DUE

4 1987			
9 2005			